WOMEN AT WORK

A Photographic Documentary

by BETTY MEDSGER

SHEED AND WARD, INC.

Subsidiary of Universal Press Syndicate

NEW YORK

To Ben, with love

Quotation on page 58 from *Mrs. Stevens Hears the Mermaids Singing,* a novel, copyright © 1965, by May Sarton, reprinted by permission of W. W. Norton & Company, Inc.
The poem on page 70, ''When I Think About Myself,'' by Maya Angelou appeared in the book *Just Give Me a Cool Drink of Water 'fore I Diiie,* published by Random House, copyright © 1971 by Hirt Music Inc.

Konica Autoreflex T3 camera used for all photographs. Photographic printing by Image, Inc., Washington, D.C. Design assistance by Dorothy Chaisson.

Library of Congress Catalog Card Number 75-1658

ISBN: 0-8362-0610-X (cloth)

0-8362-0614-2 (paper)

Introduction

The year 1974 was a special odyssey for me. I traveled throughout the United States photographing and talking with women mining coal, running corporations, taking bosses' letters, chopping down trees, stitching blue jeans and designing nuclear submarines. I did this because I wanted to document the very wide range of work being done by American women today. I wanted to convey real images of ourselves, rather than the stereotypes we regularly are fed by the mass media.

There are those who say that we have advanced too far. There are those who say we are not capable of advancing. The evidence presented by my camera, coupled with the statistics of the U.S. Department of Labor, prove that neither assumption is true.

I am not saying that every job you will see in *Women at Work* is a good job. Indeed, there is some work represented here that you may feel no living creature should be doing. Rather, *Women at Work* is a statement of what exists. I hope it will help destroy any neatly divided stereotypes of "women's work" and "men's work."

Try an experiment to test your own stereotypes. Close your eyes and think of people working. What comes to mind? Strong male shoulders, perhaps, under a blue collar and a white hard hat, hands on hips or on the controls of a crane, certainty in the eyes of the muscular man who makes the mighty machine do work for him. Or perhaps the picture that glided across your eyes was of a male surgeon in white mask and gown, barking terse orders to the small army of female nurses who surround him and make it possible for him to save heroically yet another life.

Probably few people, asked to conjure up their stereotypes of someone at work, would picture a woman surgeon ordering a scalpel from a nurse. Probably most would even have difficulty when envisioning workers to think spontaneously of those hundreds of secretaries in clerical pools at, say, the FBI, collating voluminous files, or of the thousands of women who sit in sewing factories from coast to coast, each of them a "specialist" in such things as sewing the right side of the fly of hundreds of blue jeans a day.

For many people the male construction worker and the surgeon are the *real* workers. The women who stand behind them or assist them may receive quiet admiration occasionally. But those men are emulated as the builders of society, the ones who keep the wheels turning. The women stand behind them smiling in political campaigns, obeying in operating rooms, sweating in factories. They are not seen. The men are up front where it counts—at least when it comes to the formation among children of stereotypes that remain indelible through life.

The point that diverse role models for women are still not very visible hit me again the other day when someone asked my little next-door neighbor, Julia Bailey, what she wants to be when she grows up. With the immediate and absolute certainty of age eight and one-half, Julia announced:

"I want to be a mommy and a teacher."

It could be that Julia wants to be a mommy and a teacher because of her dolls and games. She got a doll and a dollhouse for Christmas while her younger brother, Tommy, got a box of real tools.

But perhaps Julia wants to be a mommy and a teacher simply because she has two strong and good models, her mommy, Elizabeth Bailey, and her second-grade teacher, Freida Stanley. She may not realize yet that you can couple being a mommy with being just about anything else.

But as with many children and adults, it could be that Julia thinks only of being a mother and a teacher because these are virtually the only occupations she actually sees women performing. Add to teachers the occupations of nurse, salesclerk, housekeeper, stewardess, and secretary and many people's ideas of how women can earn an income is nearly exhausted.

Society continues to instill strong preconceptions that men can do anything. Whether or not we notice that men are doing an infinite variety of work we instinctively know that there is a man somewhere for every task. Simultaneously, we are taught almost from birth that many jobs either cannot or should not be done by women. We therefore believe that women can do only the things we commonly see them doing. They serve, wait, assist, sweep, nurse, adorn, and shuttle children. Even those things which society has maintained that women alone have "innate" talents for—sewing and cooking—are relinquished at the highest levels of those skills; we consider it "natural" that chefs and couturiers be men.

On the other hand, a man seen performing tasks generally allotted to women, such as child rearing, housecleaning, or teaching in a day-care center, is often considered weak and lacking in manhood. Hopefully the new humanism that should grow out of feminism will help us see work in terms of its suitability to the person rather than to the sex.

Nearly everyone has heard that there is change in the air when it comes to sex roles in work. Most people know from occasional newspaper pictures and short news stories that women wouldn't have been permitted to do some jobs ten years ago that a very few are doing now. A crane operator here, a construction worker there. A jockey here, a basketball player there. An Army pilot here, a Marine commander there.

In some newspapers the stories seem to have replaced the old two-headed cow as news space filler. They sometimes have the same freakish tone. And like the cow story, the dominant point usually is that these women are worth a glance but should not be taken seriously. Such stories go something like this:

> Susie Smith, a pert, blue-eyed blonde, is the first woman crane operator in Our Town since World War II. The men on the job laughed and said she adds a lot to the scenery at the work site.
>
> Asked if she became a crane operator to prove a point for women's lib, Miss Smith—who does not look like a women's libber and does not call herself *Ms*. Smith—smiled demurely and said, "Oh, no, I just did it because I like to operate cranes."
>
> The bright red crane nicely matched the rather snugly fitting red sweater she was wearing with her blue jeans, desert boots and orange hard hat. . . .

In the real world it's a little different. Some women, in jobs that haven't accepted women since the shortage of men during World War II, have a hell of a time. In some coal regions, for example, miners and their wives have picketed and made malicious verbal attacks on women hired to enter mines.

In Pike County, Kentucky, though, where Anita Fleming Cherry entered the mines at age thirty-nine after being a practical nurse for twenty years, there was acceptance, even if some of it was reluctant. Before long the miners elected her an officer in the local chapter of the United Mine Workers. Perhaps equally significant, while a few women in the community snickered at the idea of a woman doing "man's work," some of the older women would approach Anita and in quiet, private conversations not only pat her on the back for breaking the barrier into the mines along with miner Diana Baldwin, but also tell her of their own desires many years ago to do what she is doing now. But the world was such that they could not even have mentioned their dream—let alone think about fulfilling it.

How many dreams and simple desires have been suppressed, have made women feel they were odd when, in fact, they merely had a talent and yen that society would not accept?

Today's working women are living out a great political and human drama. The reverberations can be felt in the office, the factory, the field, and the home. There is a combination of tragedy and triumph in many working women's lives.

Some women's husbands resent their going into nontraditional work. One told me her husband hated her for it. For such women the question of husband and wife equitably sharing housecleaning and cooking could not pass the wives' lips for fear of a verbal, if not physical, battle. For others, the question is dealt with sensibly and easily.

High in a National Forest, near Mount Hood, I met a grandmother who wields a mean Pulasky, a large ax used to chop and smash stumps and big roots. She is a member of a nearly all-female slash crew that builds fire trails in the great mountains of Oregon. She and her husband both work. He cooks dinner some evenings, she cooks on other evenings. He vacuums and does other housecleaning. "He's wonderful," she says.

In the spirit of a friendly joke that's been repeated often, another member of the crew said, "Which weekend are you going to let me rent him?" Everybody laughed heartily, and then one of the women softly said, "Boy, my husband doesn't feel that way."

For Jenny Cirone, who's been lobstering in South Addison, Maine, since she was nine, it doesn't seem strange to be doing something that's done by only one other woman she knows. I think she's barely thought of it, and probably wondered why this outsider with the camera and the questions was so curious. "It's true, though, you won't find many of us," she said.

Jenny's been a permanent part of the South Addison scenery, having grown up on an island not far from the mainland. Of course, Jenny lobsters. That's Jenny and it's always been Jenny. The fishermen yell to her early the morning we set out to sea. In a deep Down East Maine accent one beckons to her to look a minute. He holds up a four-foot halibut. Jenny congratulates him. Later he will congratulate her on her lobsters, and lament that the catch isn't up to last year's. Mutual respect for mutual work.

It might be different, though, if a woman in South Addison who had not always been associated with the water and its lively riches decided to try lobstering. It's not hard to imagine a fisherman telling his forty-year-old wife contemplating such work, "Now, come on, that's men's work. No wife of mine is going to do that. You take care of the house or, if you must work, go over to Addison or Ellsworth and get a job clerking in the store." "But what about Jenny?" the wife might logically protest. "Aw, now come on, Jenny's different." "How?" the wife might ask. "Well, she just is." But in reality the wife probably knows that in most ways, save Jenny's work on the sea, they have shared the same values and life style. Both have married. Both have borne children. Both are fixtures in a landscape they love.

The same irrational arguments about sexual work stereotypes come out of the mouths of both blue collar males and white collar males.

Norma Mann, a former payroll clerk, who is president of Mann Steel Company in Dallas, the largest reinforcing steel company in the entire Southwest, heard her husband make a similar remark one day. I hasten to point out that Mr. Mann is very proud of his wife's amazing success and has given her the strongest encouragement. But one day he and Norma were having a discussion about women doing "men's work." Mr. Mann, who is an engineer was against it. Norma, instead of bringing herself up as obvious prima facie evidence, brought up Betty, another engineer in his office. "But Betty's different," he declared. "She's not like other women. She's not good because she's a woman—she's just a good engineer. Women shouldn't be engineers."

Mr. Mann, like Betty in his office, probably is a good engineer because he has developed particular mental skills completely unrelated to the fact that he has a male body. Likewise, his wife has become a leading businessperson in Dallas because she developed mental skills far beyond those required of her as a payroll clerk—a development quite irrelevant to the fact that her brain resides inside a female body.

A further irony in my experience with Norma occurred when she and her secretaries and I had a pleasant conversation about some of the new jobs women are doing. They wanted to know what pictures I had taken on my swing through the Southwest. Among them I mentioned an engineer for the Santa Fe Railroad in El Paso and a jet pilot for Braniff Airlines at the Fort Worth–Dallas Airport.

A male foreman, who was listening but not participating in the conversation, seemed to pale a little. A few minutes later as the foreman, Norma and I headed for the pickup trucks in the parking lot to visit some work sites, the foreman drawled out that he didn't think he'd be willing to ride Braniff or the Santa Fe anymore.

Even women sometimes have trouble comprehending that a job might be done according to skill, regardless of sex. In March I was taking pictures one day around a quilting frame in Buckhannon, West Virginia. Four women were stitching and chatting. Sure, they'd be glad to have their pictures taken. As I moved around, taking various angles, they, like most women I met, wanted to know about the other women in the book. I said that just the day before I had taken pictures of women coal miners.

Now, coal mining is a subject near to the hearts, and frequently the lungs, of West Virginians. So they began arguing with each other about women going inside the mines. The opponents clearly had the edge. Irene Crites summed up her position quite strongly. As she sewed the final stitches on the official state bird of some state, she declared, "That's men's work, I wouldn't want to do that. The lines for work were set a long time ago, beginning in the scriptures. There's their work and there's our work. And I think it ought to stay that way," she said with a tone of finality. A few stitches later she made the point more clearly, in case it had been missed: "Now this is our work, quilting."

Indeed, their quilting means a great deal to them. For several generations intricate patterns have been passed down to them, with each generation making adaptations and altogether new designs. Some of the quilters might be surprised, or even offended, to know that some men like to quilt. My father, unable to find work during the Depression, made quilts—not for a living, but to kill time and, in the end, he left behind some nice family heirlooms. In fact, he went to his grave with holes in his fingers, acquired because he refused to wear a thimble. At least that's what they always said. Perhaps it was because they didn't make thimbles big enough for a big man's hands.

American women have a long history of working in factories. They, like men and children, once were simply slaves in the factories of industrial barons. Too often labor reform meant removing the women and children and letting the men continue to work in the same inhumane conditions. I visited factories where gray-haired women sat stitching or cutting or grating or packing—doing tasks some of them had been repeating for up to thirty-five years. Many of them were grateful for a job. Some of them knew they had always been on the bottom rung and would never make it to the second rung and were glad some of the younger women would, though they could see some young women already stuck at the bottom rung like themselves.

Talk to a woman used to the tedium in "women's" factory work and who has just changed to a formerly male-staffed assembly line, like welding. "They keep telling me it will get boring," she says, "but I can't imagine it yet. I don't feel like a machine here." For all of them one point became clear—the "men's work," blue collar or white collar, produces a thicker roll of bills on payday. Inasmuch as many of the women who work are the sole support of themselves and their children, that factor is just as important to them as it is to male workers.

Of the 35 million women in the American labor force—45 percent of all women aged sixteen and over and 39 percent of the total labor force—a majority work because of economic need, according to data from the U.S. Bureau of the Census and the Women's Bureau of the U.S. Department of Labor.

The economic need derives from the fact that about three-fifths of all women workers are single, widowed, divorced, or separated from their husbands, or have husbands whose earnings are less than $7,000.

Among all families in the United States, one out of eight is headed by a woman. Almost three out of ten black families are headed by women. And among all poor families—those officially classified as such are the nonfarm families of four with a total annual income of less than $4,275—more than two out of five are headed by women, and almost two out of three poor black families are headed by women. A 1971 study by the Rand Corporation found that 18 percent of college-educated female heads of families were poor, compared with 3 percent of college-educated male heads of families.

Though women workers' economic needs are identical to those of the average male worker, women cannot meet those needs as well because women are still, despite innumerable attempts at good-will convincing and then lawsuits, "concentrated in low-paying deadend jobs," according to a Labor Department report. "As a result, the average woman worker earns less than three-fifths of what a man does, even when both work full time year-round."

Since 1955, when records started being kept of the differential between the median earnings of men and women who work full time, the picture has *worsened* for women. The median earnings of women working full time was 63.9 percent of the men's median earnings in 1955, 59.4 percent of men's earnings in 1970, 59.5 percent in 1971, 57.9 percent in 1972 and 56.6 percent in 1973.

Thus, in the years of "progress" in women's rights, women fell farther behind men in pay.

The Council of Economic Advisers to the President estimated in 1973 that even if adjustments were made for such factors as education, work experience during the year, and even life-long work experience, women's median earnings for full-time work even then would be 20 percent lower than the median earnings of men working full time.

Adequate analysis of this failure of women's median earnings to move toward equality of men's stymies even the experts. The Labor Department proffers this explanation: Women have been entering the labor force in greatly increasing numbers in recent years and most of them have entered at the bottom rung. Simultaneously, those who got there a little earlier have not been advancing up the ladder at the same rate as men have. Thus, the women's salaries are concentrated at the lowest levels and remain static while men receive increments at a faster pace.

Furthermore, as unemployment reached new peaks during the current recession, the unemployment rate for women was higher than that for men. In January 1975, the unemployment rate for males over twenty years of age was 6 percent. For women the comparable unemployment rate was 8.1 percent.

To add insult to injury, a woman's education does not seem to be a guaranteed ticket to equity with men. According to U.S. Census data:

Fully employed women high-school graduates have less income on the average than fully employed men who have not completed elementary school.

Fully employed women with four years of college have approximately the same income as men with an eighth-grade education.

Fully employed women with five or more years of college education have approximately the same income as men who are high-school graduates.

Like most people, the women in this book don't have those statistics on the tips of their tongues. But they have lived them.

Rita Cox, a gutsy nineteen-year-old truck driver in Los Angeles has come to symbolize for me the incredible capacity of women to change their lives. She did it by sheer force of desire combined with need. Not until after her struggles and after she was beginning to be successful did she start to philosophize about it.

I was waiting in the dispatcher's station at an asphalt hauling company in Santa Fe Springs, California. I was told Rita Cox would be right in. I saw this slim woman with long and high teased black hair come toward the building. It never entered my mind that she might be Rita the truck driver. I guess I thought she was a secretary to the dispatcher. Obviously, though I hate to admit it, I had a stereotype of what a woman truck driver would look like, and this wasn't it.

"Hi, I'm Rita. I hear you want to take my picture. What's your book about?" I explained my project and she thought it was cool. "Why don't you go out on my run today, then you can really see what it's like," suggested Rita as she hit each of the giant tires of her diesel rig with an iron bar, a normal safety precaution taken by each driver at the beginning of her or his shift.

Why not? By that time I had already climbed up high metal catwalks and stood before dynamite blasts in a coal mine and the open hearth of a steel mill—places that before I began this book I would have gone willingly only at gunpoint. I had been chased out of a California celery field by a farm manager who thought I was an agitator for the United Farm Workers Union. While photographing a police sergeant on patrol duty in the highest crime district of Washington, D.C., we responded to a report that a man had been found with his head cut off. So, a ride around the freeways of Los Angeles in the cab of a Mack diesel double trailer seemed like small beans.

There I was, camera around my neck, feet on the dashboard in the middle of rush-hour traffic, about to hear the incredible life story of Rita Cox.

She was a high-school dropout at fourteen. "I was the kind of kid that was always getting into trouble. Somebody told me one of my old teachers said not long ago that she couldn't believe I'd ever settle down to anything, least of all being a truck driver."

Actually, Rita had to settle down pretty fast after she dropped out of school. She was married and had a son shortly after she left school. The marriage was soon rocky and she and her husband separated. Rita says that just about all the women she went to school with dropped out early, married, had children, were divorced and are now on welfare by age nineteen. "They all stay at home. They say to me, 'Gee, Rita, that's great what your doing.' I say, 'If I can do it so can you.' That really bugs me. Here I am now paying for their welfare when they could go out and get good jobs too. It doesn't pay me to work too much overtime because it all goes to the welfare."

Rita doesn't know why she didn't fall into the same pattern as her friends. She wanted to work from the beginning. First she wrapped meat at a couple of different supermarkets. While she was a meat wrapper she was dating a trucker. "He had a beautiful truck. He was so proud of it. It was all white and chrome inside," she said, fingering the inside of the roof of her own rig. "He used to tell me all about it, took me for rides. His rig meant a lot to him. I got to like it, too. Then I told him I wanted to be a trucker. From then on he wouldn't tell me anymore about the truck and things got bad between us. He said a woman couldn't drive a truck. That's not true, of course. . . .

"Every place I went for a job they'd say, 'See you later.' They wouldn't even give me a road test. And they seemed to think it was awfully funny that I wanted to be a trucker."

Like many women breaking into nontraditional jobs, at the time Rita was trying to break the barrier she was not thinking much about the fact that she was doing something unusual. She was simply determined to do something she liked. She also knew that as a trucker she would make $7.54 an hour. As a meat wrapper she was making $4.49 an hour.

And although she thought wrapping meat was a drag, she thought driving a truck was terrific. The fact that she was doing something unusual was forced on her consciousness by others' reactions.

For would-be women truck drivers the difficulty begins when you find there is virtually no place to learn to drive a rig. It's a skilled job and requires some lessons. Maneuvering a double diesel rig is a far cry from maneuvering the family station wagon. Trucking schools are often reluctant to take women. They say the reluctance is based on the fact that they have trouble getting jobs for women. So, the determined woman finds another "school."

"The way it is now," said Rita, "the only way a woman around here can learn to be a trucker if her man isn't a trucker is to go to a truck stop and say, 'Hey, let me drive your truck to Pomona so I can learn to drive and I'll give you what you want.' Then when you get to Pomona you hide from him or run away when he's not looking and after a while hitchhike back to L.A.

"It's a terrible way, but what's a woman to do? That's why some other women and I are trying to get funds to start a training school for women truck drivers."

Like so many of the women I photographed in nontraditional jobs, she belies the stereotypes reflected by such corner of the mouth comments as I heard occasionally from men during my odyssey: "Are you taking pictures of that kind of woman, too?"

Well, Rita knows and cares desperately about that sterotype: "I think it's important to be feminine. You may have noticed that I try to look feminine." Yes, in addition to the teased hair, I couldn't help noticing the long false eyelashes and lots of makeup. "I think the most important thing to a woman is to have pride in herself. If she doesn't have that, she doesn't have anything. . . .

"It's tough, I meet new guys and they find out I'm a trucker and they say, 'Oh, you're a women's libber' and walk away. I'm hurt by that. I'm not trying to compare with any man. You know women were created from men's ribs, after all. Anyhow, so I got that I'd not tell anybody what I did until after they knew me pretty well. Instead, I'd lie and tell them I was a meat wrapper or a secretary or a hair stylist. But the guy I'm going with now I met on New Year's Eve, and when he asked me what I did, I thought, 'Damn it, I'm going to tell him.' He just kind of laughed and said, 'Outta sight,' and things have been fine with us.''

Listening to Rita for several hours was an audio kaleidoscope. Every view she expressed about herself seemed to collide with a conflicting reaction that would come out of her later. And yet there she was, seeming to put it all together much more coherently than many white-collar women I had met or read.

"I really love trucking," she said. "At first I got so tired that I'd wonder why I was doing this to myself, but I got over that. Besides, diesel fuel gets in your blood. You know, if I get married again it's going to have to be a trucker so we can drive cross-country together. Wouldn't that be a good way to live?'' Inasmuch as my husband and I were then traveling together cross-country working on separate journalistic projects, I agreed that, yes, that was a good way to live.

Our time together had begun at four in the afternoon. We had driven north to Pomona to pick up a load of asphalt and then driven south, nearly to Long Beach, to dump it. We had learned a lot about each other by the time we had dumped the asphalt and were returning to the dispatcher's station. She had asked a lot of questions about the other women in the book, and seemed very excited about being included in a documentary of working women. She was astonished that a woman could actually be a policewoman. (A policeman had told her that wouldn't be good.)

"By the way," she asked suddenly as we drove along the dark freeway, "Do most of the women in your book belong to the women's liberation movement?'' She had already told me that she was insulted when men accused her of being part of women's liberation. I was surprised by the question and said it was a hard one to answer. I said I thought most of the women I had talked to probably were not part of any women's liberation organizations, but that a majority of them had been affected by the movement, sometimes without even being conscious of what had happened to them. There was a pregnant pause while I got up the nerve to hesitantly suggest, "I suspect maybe that's even true for you.''

Immediately she said, "That's right. For instance, some nights I work twelve hours and don't get home 'til 5 A.M. And then a few hours later my boyfriend might come in and ask me to fix him a sandwich. Now I tell him, 'Look, I'm not trying to compare with you, but I worked twelve hours last night and I'm tired. You have two hands, make your own sandwich.' Not long ago I wouldn't have done that.''

Sometimes it was as revealing to listen to the people who supervise or manage women workers as it was to talk to the workers themselves.

In a sewing factory, the only man in the place besides the owner was a supervisor who was young enough to be the grandson of some of the women bent over the sewing machines, positions their bodies had held for twenty to thirty years in this small, rural town. Very authoritatively the young man, hands on hips and surveying the room from the front, said that these women could do "pretty well." Why, they could start at a dollar and something an hour, he said, and, if they worked hard, they could advance to two dollars and something an hour after a couple of years. He added that the company didn't get much out of them until they had been there awhile.

In Hollywood I heard a similar attitude in more glamorous surroundings.

A woman who models because she wants to make money so she can pursue her real love, acting, without starving, told me how "modeling is really an insult to your intelligence. There's no challenge, no creativity in it."

A little more than an hour later, after the model's shooting session, I was being driven through Beverly Hills in a Thunderbird by a man and woman who manage models.

He: She really knows how to move.

She: Yes, she does.

He: Europe has done absolute marvels for her.

She: It sure has.

He: (having switched the discussion to another model under their tutelage) It was just a year ago August that she started making it.

She: Yes, it happened so fast. She may be the next very big one.

He: It's really something. Her mother is just a simple factory worker. This July she took her mother to Europe for the first time, and she has bought herself a Porsche.

She: You feel good about a girl like that. She really enjoys her money, spends it well.

He: Yeah, if we could just get her to work more often.

There are more than 170 different occupations represented in this book. I do not rank them according to importance. But I would like to single out one woman as the most important woman in the book: Sharon Epps.

Sharon made me cry. She is the only person who did that during my odyssey into the world of working women. My camera and I were witnesses to her entrance into the world. Sure, I know the event of birth happens a few thousand times an hour. But viewing it for the first time was a great occasion. It seemed appropriate in those moments of her dramatic entrance into Mississippi for a symphony orchestra to play grand triumphant welcome strains, for a giant chorus to shout "Hallelujah, Sharon is here!"

In a way that's what happened. I had come to take a picture of Nancy Umphers, a nurse-midwife, helping to bring a new baby into the world. Irene Epps had been walking to work at her factory job the same day I drove into town and her pains started coming. She got herself to the hospital and we all waited until more than twenty-four hours later when the pace of the pains announced that the new Epps family member would make the scene soon.

In the end, my *Women at Work* pictures that day included not just midwife, but also mother, both very much at work. Through prenatal care each had known the other for some months by that time. So, when Irene was suffering, she would call Nancy by her first name, "Nancy, Nancy, help me, please."

I had chosen a spot in the delivery room where it seemed I would be able to get the best pictures and be in nobody's way. I could see everything. Nancy has delivered a lot of babies, but here she was after many hours of Irene's pain and work, literally beaming as she gently helped the baby out and nearly shouted in happiness, "Hey, Irene, we got us a beautiful baby!" The baby did not need the proverbial spank on the bottom to let us all know that she had sturdy lungs.

Nancy held her high and Irene leaned up as far as one could after that much work. And there was the symphony welcome on her face. I am not ashamed to say that because of quietly spilling tears, I wasn't quite sure if that picture was in focus until I saw the negative.

Undoubtedly the meaning of the moment of Sharon's birth was increased by the fact that Nancy Umphers had told me that she had just ten years ago been a leading force in trying to get a private school established so her children wouldn't have to go to school with black children. All that has changed and now her life is committed to helping the poor of Holmes County—invariably black people—enter the world on a healthy and, therefore, a little more nearly equal footing with the other citizens of the county. The changes within Nancy have sometimes been painful. The changes have been bolstered by a conviction that such a life is morally right but pained by the fact that sometimes people near and dear to her do not share her convictions.

After a few minutes Irene was wheeled from the delivery room, accompanied by Nancy and the attending nurse. The door was closed. Sharon and I were alone. I pulled up a very short footstool and sat on it in front of her incubator. We were eye to eye. She was on her side and seemed to be looking at me. I forgot whatever I knew about how long it takes a baby's eyes to focus, for I was sure she was staring at me—and smiling yet. I took a few pictures of her there in the incubator. But mostly I just looked at her and thought of the complicated and difficult world she would be entering.

I thought about the fact that that night I would be staying at the home of a woman publisher in Lexington whom the Ku Klux Klan had once plotted to kill because she stood for equal rights for all. Sharon probably would grow up in that community.

I thought about the fact that Sharon was black and a woman. Black feminists call that a double whammy. It is in a society that has not yet obliterated the vestiges of slavery it has forever attached to women and black people of both sexes.

And then I hoped that when Sharon reached the age of reason she wouldn't be forced to choose only from among occupations that society has declared to be either "black folks' work" or "women's work," but that she would be able to choose work that she simply liked and was capable of doing.

I wished then and now for a better world for Sharon and all the other new women, whether they are literally just coming out of the womb, or be they twenty, forty, fifty, or sixty years old and just now emerging from the unyielding wombs in which our society has held them.

Betty Medsger

Washington, D.C.
February 1975

SOURCES

Current unemployment rates were provided by the Bureau of Labor Statistics, U.S. Department of Labor, Washington, D.C.

The Rand Corporation Report cited is "Non-Support of Legitimate Children by Affluent Fathers as a Cause of Poverty and Welfare Dependence," Rand Corporation, Santa Monica, California, 1971.

The following statistical sources were published by the Employment Standards Administration, Women's Bureau, U.S. Department of Labor, Washington, D.C.: "Fact Sheet on Earnings Gap," "Twenty Facts on Women Workers," "Highlights of Women's Employment and Education," "Why Women Work," "Women Workers Today," "Median Earnings of Full-Time Year-Round Workers, by Sex, 1955-72," "Facts on Women Workers of Minority Races," and "The Myth and the Reality."

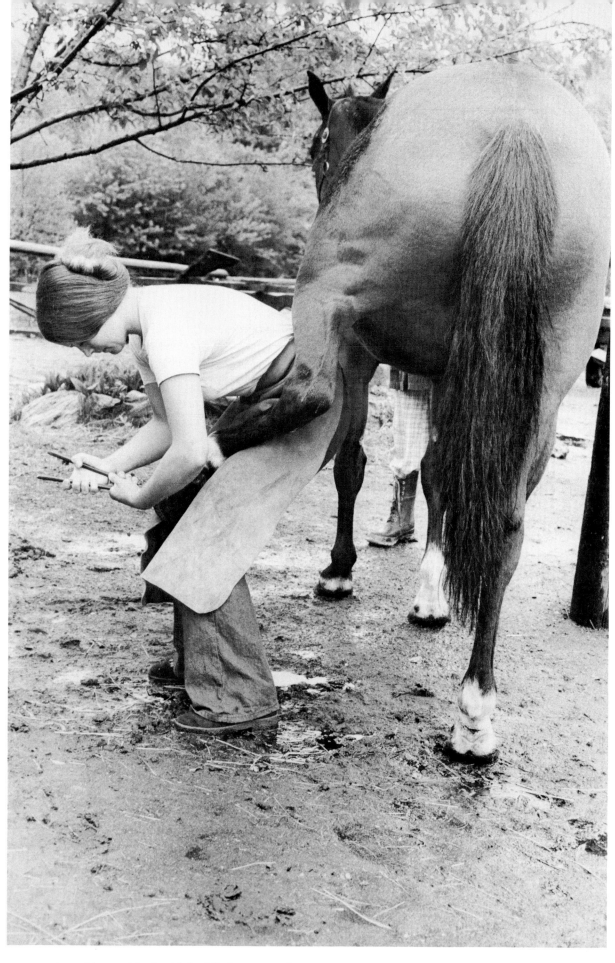

Janet Murray, blacksmith in Billerica, Massachusetts.

Scottie Wiest, potter in Rock Cave, West Virginia.

Linda Miller, heavy equipment operator at the
Alamitos Generating Station, Long Beach, California.

"I think some of the men here at the station didn't
like the idea at first. But after they saw I was doing a
good job, they were okay. My father is probably
responsible for my wanting to do a different kind of
work. He thought it was a man's world and that a girl
should know how to do as much as possible to get
along. So, when I was growing up it was as natural
for me to change the oil in the car as it was to do the
dishes."—*Linda Miller.*

"It's fun seeing their little minds grow, especially when they're this young. One to six is fine for me. I don't want to teach the older children. With the young children you can see them learning, watch their faces respond. They make you feel you've accomplished something by the end of the day."
—*Freida Stanley*.

Freida Stanley, second grade teacher, Janney School, Washington, D.C.

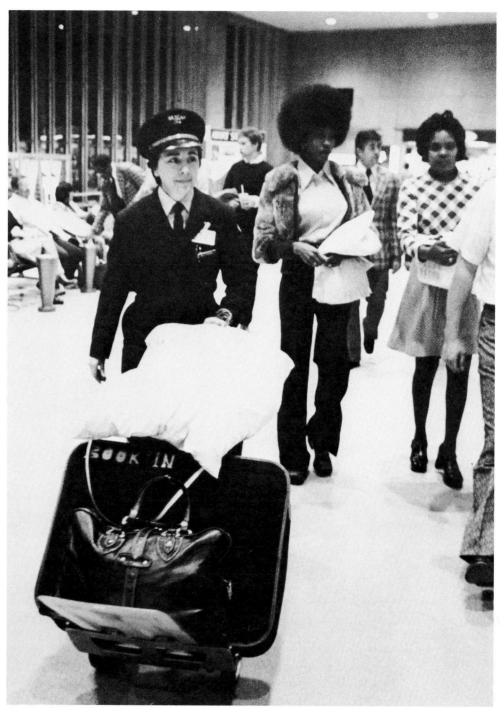

Nelly Fernandez, skycap at National Airport,
Alexandria, Virginia.

"In Argentina I was a sewing teacher. . . . I did a little
of that in this country when I came here. I originally
came to the airport to work in security. They asked me
to do this, and I like it. . . . Understand, it is not my
dream job, but I like it."—*Nelly Fernandez.*

Air Force Lt. Catherine N. Bugg, aircraft maintenance officer at Barksdale Air Force Base, Louisiana, a Strategic Air Command base; supervises 560 people.

"My husband has been in the Air Force several years. We kept moving every time he was reassigned. I didn't have a chance to get very deeply into anything that way, so I decided to beat it by joining up too. . . .

"I have very few problems with being a woman in such a nearly all male world. There's been absolutely no problem with the ground crews, who are beneath me in rank. I have had some problems with the pilots. In Guam they yelled some pretty bad things at me from the windows of their buses as they were being taken to their B52's. . . . It's interesting, they can accept us in positions superior to them better than they can in positions equal to them. . . .

"I'm very proud of the fact that I was fully qualified to be stationed in Guam in time to okay the last B52's that bombed Cambodia."—*Air Force Lt. Catherine N. Bugg.*

Dr. Elaine R. Wedral, left, food chemist and new products development coordinator for Libby-McNeill Foods, and Joyce R. Anderson, food engineer, at Chicago plant.

Trisha Pennock, interior designer with Wall and Window, Hyde Park, Chicago.

The woman who owns this high-rise apartment in the northern suburbs of Chicago instructed her interior decorator: "I want it to be the kind of place that when people open the door they'll go, 'AhhhHHHhhh, My GOD!' "

Dorothy Morgan, worker in So Others May Eat (Some House) soup kitchen in Washington, D.C.

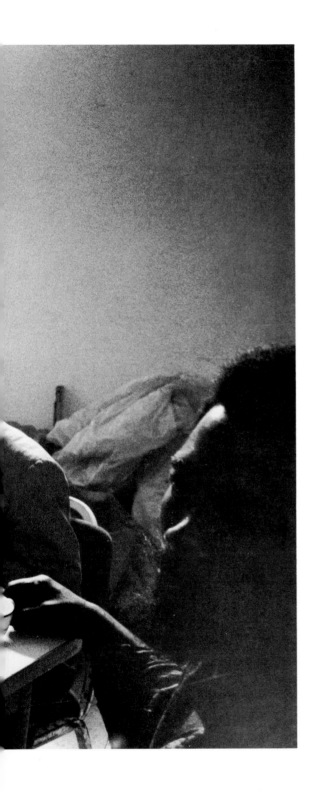

"It means a lot to me to work here. I'm here seven days a week. I used to be down and out myself. I've been in this soup line many times. I'm all right now. I cook in the mornings, help serve the meals later in the day. It's the only way I can keep my feet on the ground. This is my peace."—*Dorothy Morgan.*

Betty Williams, street cleaner for Solid Waste
Management Administration, Washington, D.C.

The Rockette dancers at Radio City Music Hall, New York City.

Cynthia Bates, cement mason in Washington, D.C.

Retha Gambaro, sculptor, Washington, D.C.

"I can spend whole days out here in my studio and never feel alone. There's something in the stone, and I'm discovering it, watching it develop. It becomes my companion."—*Retha Gambaro.*

Martha J. Sloan, bus driver for Metro Bus,
Washington, D.C.

Martha Sloan works a split shift. She drives the rush hours in early morning and late afternoon. In her free time she is a counselor at the Washington, D.C., Rape Crisis Center.

"People still say something once in a while about the 'woman bus driver,' but there are quite a few of us now. . . . When I was being trained, my long hair bothered some people. One day a woman approached my trainer, a man, and she said to him—even though I was right there and she could've said it to me—'You tell that young woman that if she's going to do a man's job she should cut her hair and look like a man.' "—*Martha Sloan.*

**Janet Ressler spinning wool to use on her loom in
Penobscot, Maine.**

Wilma Ann Jancuk, chemical engineer in inorganic finishing, development engineering and environmental studies at Western Electric's Hawthorne Plant, Cicero, Illinois.

A typing pool at the J. Walter Thompson Advertising and Public Relations Agency, New York City.

Every summer Brucie Riggs hikes in the Oregon wilderness as a ranger for five days. Then she comes out for two days, takes a warm shower, catches up on the news, eats at least one Mexican meal and returns to the wilderness for another five days.

"I meet about sixty people a day along the trail. Sometimes they need information. Sometimes they get lost and want help, like the Boy Scout Troop that got split here a few weeks ago. . . . I also pick up garbage in the woods. Some men are surprised. They size me up and say, 'What are you doing here?' . . . I have a French degree, but I'm going back to college now for a degree in biology. Working summers in the wilderness convinced me I want to work outside all the time studying plants or animals."—*Brucie Riggs*.

Brucie Riggs, wilderness ranger for the National Forest Service in the Detroit Range District in Oregon.

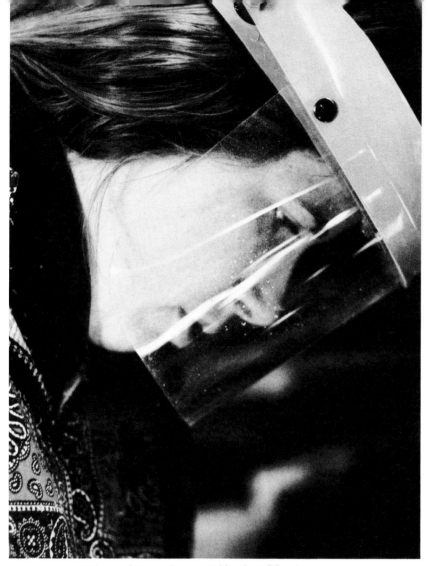

Lee Wiley, cabinetmaker in Oakland, California.

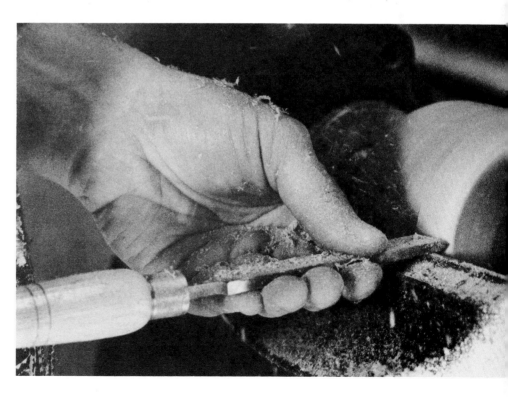

Data processors for American Security Bank, Washington, D.C.

Lucinda Keller, house painter, Cambridge, Massachusetts.

Elizabeth Cotton, veteran folk singer and songwriter (wrote "Freight Train") who lives in Washington, D.C. Concert is on campus of Duke University, Durham, North Carolina.

Beatrice W. Babica, forklift operator at Hawthorne Plant of Western Electric, Cicero, Illinois.

Ione Conolley, quilter on Route 5, Buckhannon, West Virginia. Behind her is her grandmother, Mary Leota Hinkle, age eighty-eight, and in front is her daughter, Martha, age three.

The quilting frame was standing, as usual, in front of the big window in the living room so the sun could offer the greatest help to Ione Conolley's tiny stitches. At least the third generation of quilters in her family, Mrs. Conolley is expert at creating original quilt designs. Now she sews quilts designed by a highly paid designer in New York who works for Mountain Artisans. A plastic bag of patches chosen by the designer arrived as I photographed her. It was Friday and she was to complete the quilt by Tuesday for delivery to New York. She would be paid $35 to $40 for such a quilt. In leading department and gift stores, the Mountain Artisans firm sells the quilts made by West Virginia women for up to $800.

Amanda Oestreich, bunny, Playboy Club, Chicago,
Illinois.

I learned something new about the work done by bunnies the night I toured the Chicago Playboy Club with one of the club's public relations agents. We ran into Joey on the Penthouse level.

> JOEY: Pat, I'm glad to see you. I want you to do me a favor. My cousin goes to college down in Terre Haute—you know, the federal prison down there. He's on the entertainment committee and he'd like to have some of the girls come down to the prison in costume.

> P. R. AGENT: No, Joey. We can't do that.

> JOEY: Whatsamatter? You don't like those guys, got something against them? It would get him some good credit with the guards if he could bring the girls down.

> P. R. AGENT: Joey, they're not going. You know what the policy is. We only allow the girls to go to veterans' hospitals and orphanages.

A Navy officer said he thought things were "changing fast in regard to women in the military. About the only area where they are absolutely prohibited is combat. And that will drop eventually, I'm sure.

"But I'll be honest with you. I wouldn't want my wife or daughter going into combat. But then I wouldn't want my son going into combat either."—*Navy Lt. George C. Gillett, Jr.,* Public Information Division officer at the Pentagon, May 1974.

**Army Pvt. Peggy L. Swisher, military policewoman at
Fort Jackson, Columbia, South Carolina.**

Judy Braley, skeiner at Bartlett Yarns, Inc., Harmony, Maine.

Policewomen began working on patrol duty in Washington, D.C., in 1972. Proud of their performance Police Chief Jerry V. Wilson told the *New York Times* two years later, "...You cannot classify people on the basis of sex. I think it's possible to have a police force of all women, and I would be willing to run it."

In Washington it became clear that policewomen do the same things policemen do and have the same things done to them, even in the extreme. In July 1974 a Washington policewoman shot and killed a suspect whom she thought was about to attempt to kill her and others. In August a Washington policewoman was shot and killed as she confronted a bank robbery suspect.

But policewomen seem to have one asset that benefits not only them but policemen and society in general. A 1972 book-length study, *Women and Policing*, by the Police Foundation, studied sex-integrated police departments in seven cities and concluded that there is a "reduction in the incidence of violence when women are assigned to patrol." The study also concluded that policewomen "tend to defuse volatile situations and provoke less hostility than men."

Sgt. Mary Ellen Albrecht, on patrol with the
Metropolitan Police Department, Washington, D.C.

For many years, there have been efforts to outlaw the use of the short hoe in California's fields. It has been outlawed in many other states because of the serious back injuries it causes to the women, men, and children who use it. But the growers' lobby in California has always been successful in getting the measure defeated in the state legislature. They say the workers do better work if their eyes are close to the ground.

Carmen Gallardo, field hand near Santa Maria,
California.

**Cannery workers at Stayton Canning, Brooks #5
plant, Salem, Oregon.**

"I knew there were no other women doing it in the
United States. But that fact didn't matter. I sort of
wished I was French and male, but my love for cooking
transcended the barriers. There was no choice to be
made: I was going to become a chef.

"I see food in terms of art, and for me this is an
extension of my original love of painting. I graduated
from Macalester College with a major in art, and then
worked with an ad agency. But after my daughter was
born, I became obsessed with cooking. . . .

"My progress has been very fast. I got to be a saucier
at the Waldorf [Astoria Hotel], which is usually
considered the highest level among chefs. . . . But to be
the purest, finest kind of master chef I want to be may
take ten to fifteen years."—*Leslie Arp.*

Leslie Arp, chef at P.S. 77, a French restaurant in New York City.

Sandra Simmons, pilot with Braniff Airlines, based in Dallas, Texas.

"I'm a second officer on turbo jets now. I'll be the first female to check out as first officer on jet equipment. . . . My children are excited about it. My husband told me that one day when he and the girls dropped me off at the airport, Andrea, who is nine, watched me go away from the car, and said, 'There goes a great lady.'

". . . The pilots have been wonderful. One openly had said he thought a cockpit was no place for a woman. But even he has been very good about it. That's important because they could create so much heat when we're out there that they could force me to fail.—*Sandra Simmons.*

Second Officer Simmons checks out the exterior of the jet craft as part of preparation for takeoff.

Denise F. Yorkshire, air traffic controller at National Airport, Alexandria, Virginia.

Maggi Fenerty, front, and Joan Simms, United Airlines
stewardesses on a flight from Washington, D.C., to
Chicago.

Esther Webber, shoe lining trimmer, Kesslen Shoe Factory, Kennebunk, Maine.

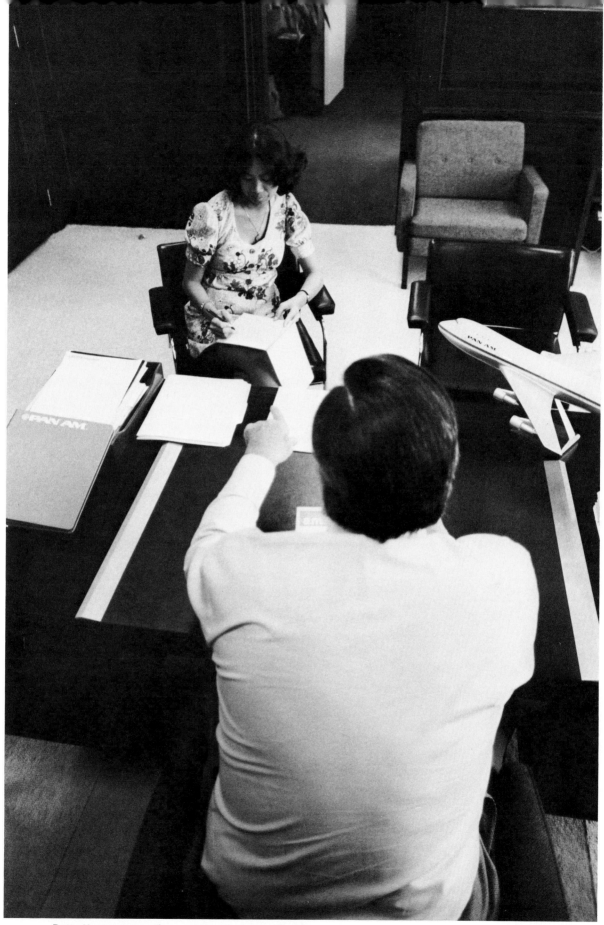

Betty Kwong, executive secretary in international services division of Pan American World Airways, New York City.

Lydia Selby, leather worker in Kanawha Head, West Virginia.

Lydia Selby crafts leather belts and purses on the small farm she and her husband moved to from Richmond, Va. In the city she worked in a leather shop. ''People would come in and think I was a clerk instead of someone who worked with leather. When they learned that I was one of the workers, they would ask that their order not be made by 'the woman.' '' Working at home now eliminates that problem. Lydia was looking forward to selling the fruit of a winter and spring's work at the annual Strawberry Festival in Buckhannon, W. Va. She thought her baby would be born about festival time.

"I've been on the linotype since 1945. I started out in Columbia, S. C. We had two kinds of high schools there, the ones that prepared you for college and the ones that gave you on-the-job training. I knew I'd never go to college, so I went to the other one. I was being trained as a secretary to a small job printer. The boss came to me after I'd been there a short time and said, 'You're going to have to learn how to operate the linotype.' All the men were going to the war. Well, I was so upset I went home and cried all night. I wanted to be a secretary. . . .

"I'm happy it happened that way. I came to love it. I'm much better off being a linotype operator. I even married one. Of course, after the war they didn't want women, wanted rid of us. We had to fight to stay on then. We also had to fight to get in the union."—*Lerline M. Santos.*

Lerline M. Santos, linotype operator in the patent
composing room of the Government Printing Office,
Washington, D.C.

Deborah J. Dale, florist at Lee's Florist, Berkeley,
California.

Meat packers at King Foods, St. Paul, Minnesota.

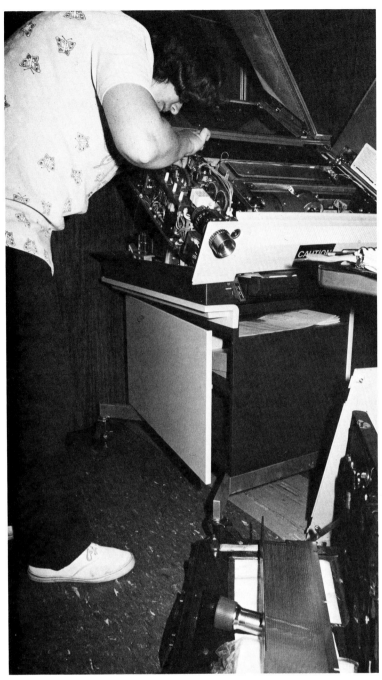

Judy Shiner, Xerox repairer, Englewood, Colorado.

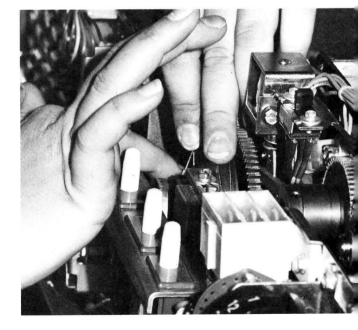

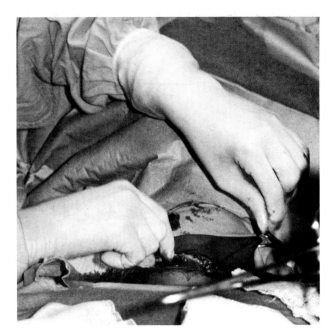

Dr. Julieta D. Grosh, surgeon at Temple University
Hospital, Philadelphia, Pennsylvania.

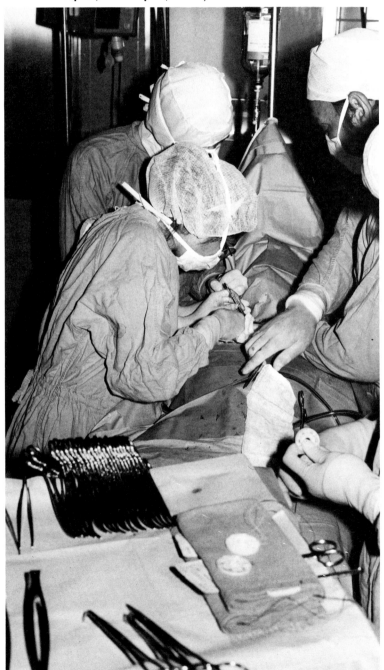

". . . Trapped by life. There was, even at seventy, no escape. One did one's work against a steady barrage of demands, of people . . . and the garden too! (It was high time she thought about sowing seeds.) It was all very well to insist that art was art and had no sex, but the fact was that the days of men were not in the same way fragmented, atomized by indefinite small tasks. There was such a thing as woman's work and it consisted chiefly, Hilary sometimes thought, in being able to stand constant interruption and keep your temper. Each single day she fought a war to get to her desk before her little bundle of energy had been dissipated, to push aside or cut through an intricate web of slight threads pulling her in a thousand directions—that unanswered letter, that telephone call . . . ''—from *Mrs. Stevens Hears the Mermaids Singing*, a novel by May Sarton.

May Sarton, novelist and poet, York, Maine.

Sharon Prah, mother, Washington, D.C.

"I think Jennifer and Heidi are much more independent because I've always worked. . . . Our home is not child centered. You might say that our children have had to adjust to us instead of us adjusting to them. They go every place with us. They do the things we like to do. For instance, we're volleyball freaks, and we take them with us once a week to play volleyball."

Sharon Prah, in addition to being the mother of Heidi and Jennifer and wife of Harry—with whom she shares household duties—is a school librarian. When she and Harry remodeled their home, she did the electric wiring.

"I hope my children see me as a person capable of doing several things well, not just as the cook or the person who can take care of them. Understand, I want them to see me as a caring, loving person. But their seeing me as a whole person is really important to me."

Marine Col. Mary E. Bane is the first woman battalion commander of men in the Marine Corps. As commanding officer of Headquarters and Service Battalion at Camp Pendleton, she has approximately 2,150 Marines under her command.

"I see no point in my having my picture taken for this book, and, frankly, I consider it a waste of my time. But they made me promise not to be rude to you. . . .

"I'm sorry, but I had to take that telephone call. The caller is a very busy man. And so am I. Or rather, I am a busy woman."

Col. Mary E. Bane, Marine battalion commander at
Camp Pendleton, California.

"I don't ride to beat the boys, just to win," said Denise Boudrot, jockey at Suffolk Downs in Boston. Her policy must be working. She was the leading rider for the 1974 season at Suffolk Downs. As such her total purse was $275,226, and she became the first woman to be "top jock" at a major race track.

Fellow Suffolk jockey Barbara Smith said that when she and Denise started racing at Suffolk, "People wouldn't bet on us. They hollered from the stands, 'Go home and wash dishes.' Then Denise won on some long shots and people started thinking we were good luck."

Both women were on the money in every race they ran on my day at the races.

Denise M. Boudrot, jockey at Suffolk Downs, Boston, Massachusetts.

Anita Fleming Cherry, coal miner in Virgie, Kentucky.

Anita Cherry leaves the mine after a night's work.

Russell Fleming worked in the coal mines for thirty years. It was the best work around Pike County, but it was rough work. He always said he didn't want his sons to work in the mines. Neither of them did.

But his daughter, Anita, did.

At age thirty-nine in 1973, Anita Fleming Cherry started working in Mine #29 in Virgie, Kentucky. It all began one day when Anita was visiting her parents and a friend of the family mentioned that "the company" was accepting applications from women, even to go into the mines. Anita thought that strange. "Why do women want to go into the mines?" she asked. The visitor said, "I guess because they can make forty to fifty dollars a day." Anita said, "Well, heck, I'll try it for that." She left twenty years of practical nursing and entered the mines. On that day she doubled her daily salary.

"Sure, some people object to us being here," she said early one morning inside the mine, "but you'd be surprised at the older women who tell me they wish they could've done this when they were young."

Warehouse workers at Montgomery Ward, Chicago.

Pamela Waters, industrial designer, in lobby she designed in New York City.

When I think about myself,
I almost laugh myself to death,
My life has been one great big joke,
A dance that's walked
A song that's spoke,
I laugh so hard I almost choke
When I think about myself.

Sixty years in these folks' world
The child I works for calls me girl
I say "Yes ma'am" for working's sake.
Too proud to bend
Too poor to break,
I laugh until my stomach ache,
When I think about myself.

My folks can make me split my side,
I laughed so hard I nearly died,
The tales they tell, sound just like lying,
They grow the fruit,
But eat the rind,
I laugh until I start to crying,
When I think about my folks.

"When I Think About Myself"
by Maya Angelou

Geneva Williamson, household worker, Washington, D.C.

By 7 A.M., when the fishing is good, the women are lined up at the work tables in O'Hara's fish plant and working hard. It's dependable work about half the year. They turn on their radios at home about 5 A.M. every day to hear whether they will work that day.

About a dozen of the women invited me to their coffee break and chatted about their work and mine, too. The idea of women working outside the home is as common an idea as daybreak to these women. "Most women around here work," said one who has been working at one fish plant or another for many years. "You got to today to get along. One salary's not enough."

Linda Cross, fish cutter at F. J. O'Hara & Sons, Inc., fish plant, Rockland, Maine.

Julie Gross, painter, New York City.

Vibeke Trusty, salesclerk at Harzfeld's Department Store, Kansas City, Missouri.

"Actually, I was trained as a physiologist. I do this because it's part time and it suits the schedules of my husband and Kim, my four-year-old daughter. I work eleven to four and then I'm home to prepare his dinner in plenty of time. . . . It's pleasant work, but I don't have to use my head at all. I wouldn't want to do it for many years."—*Vibeke Trusty.*

Donna Rueger, draftswoman operating Rembrain, a computer graphics machine, at Western Electric's Central Region Headquarters in Rolling Meadows, Illinois.

Front to rear, assistant foreman June Sears, Carolyn
Wolfe, Agnes R. Brown, Mabel Woods, and Marie
McGinnis, all workers on a slash crew in Mount
Hood National Forest in Oregon.

76

**Jessamine Durante, vice president, Harris Trust
Savings Bank, and administrator of its personal
banking division, Chicago, Illinois.**

In 1971, after forty years on the staff of Harris Trust Savings
Bank, Jessamine Durante was made a vice president of the
bank. For many years she specialized in handling the accounts
of rich women. "You know, I don't believe my being a woman
ever had anything to do with anything that happened to me in
my career."

Nancy Quinn, teller at an American Security branch
bank, Washington, D.C.

Jayne Leyser, landscape artist, Atlanta, Georgia.

Virginia D. Christian, a nuclear project engineer who
does structural analyses on nuclear submarines for
the Navy at General Dynamics/Electric Boat, Groton,
Connecticut.

Victoria Bond, orchestra conductor, at the Cabrillo
Music Festival, Aptos, California.

"Traditionally the roles of women in authority have been the teacher and
the mother. Both are roles where she is the elder and derives her
authority from age. The conductor traditionally has been anything but a
mother figure. The conductor is much more like a general than a mother
or teacher. It's a kind of enforced leadership, the kind of leadership more
likely to be expected of men than women.

"A woman conductor, because of those traditions, must rely completely
on being able to transmit authority purely on the grounds of her musical
ability. There are so few of us that we have no traditions. . . .

"At the Cabrillo Festival this summer one of the violinists came up to
me after a rehearsal and said, 'I've never played under a woman before.'
I asked him if it was any different than playing under a man. That
seemed to stop him a moment, then he said, 'No, it isn't. You are a good
musician.' "—Victoria Bond.

"I love these animals. They are my whole life now. There are fifty-one horses in this particular field. I know every one of them, and all the young ones are the product of my work. . . .I hated the modeling scene in New York. I had no friends among those people. My only friends were horse people who lived out from the city. Not everyone understands why I gave it up for this, but how could anyone look at this place and not understand it? . . . My mother thinks I'm crazy for leaving modeling for this. I went home at Easter for one day, and the first thing she said was, 'My God! What happened to your nails?' "—*Carol Eastman.*

Carol Eastman, horse breeder and rancher at Cauble Ranches, Denton, Texas.

**Andrea Mitchell Jackson, City Hall reporter for KYW
radio and television, Philadelphia, Pennsylvania.**

Linda Daly married a clown a couple of years ago. His father was a clown and so was his grandfather. So, as soon as her daughter, Shannon, was born, Linda followed the Daly family tradition and became a clown.

"I love it. We have our own show, clowning and trampolines. I don't think I could be a plain housewife after doing this. It's nice being part of a circus.

"But there's one thing I don't like about clowning. I think every woman kind of wants to be a woman, don't you? Well, it bothers me every time I see the other girls putting on their makeup and looking pretty. I have to dress up like a man and go out and act like a man. People want clowns to be men even when they are women."—*Linda Daly*, in dressing room at Capital Centre, Landover, Md.

Georgie Virshup, chair caner, French Creek, West Virginia.

Her boss told me, "We've got just the little girl for you. She's cute, weighs barely one hundred pounds, and I think she's going to do all right."

The "little girl" turned out to be thirty-three years old, supported four children ages seven through fourteen, and had been delivering mail for six and a half years.

"I was a waitress in a cafeteria at the Pentagon before I came to the post office. As you can imagine, this is a lot better. . . .I work out in the open and I'm pretty much my own boss. There's no one breathing down your back. I know most of the people on my route, and they know me and depend on me."—*Mary Alston*.

Mary Alston, postal carrier, Bethesda, Maryland.

Elaine Mezzio, candlemaker at Stone Candles,
Oakland, California.

"I work on farm animals in the morning and do surgery in the afternoon. I've been practicing for fifteen years, and there's been almost no reaction to the idea of a woman vet. I think that's because farm men are so used to their women doing about half the farm work anyhow, so I guess they don't think anything about it when they see a woman taking care of their animals."—*Dr. Nedra Carpenter.*

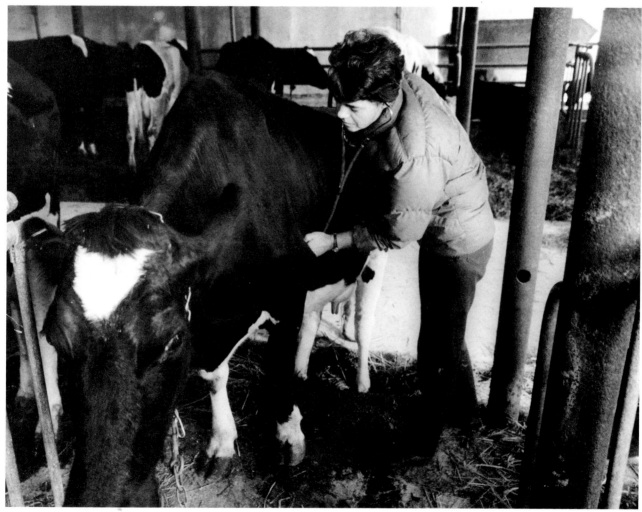

Dr. Nedra Carpenter, veterinarian, Everett, Pennsylvania.

Dr. Claire Fishman, clinical psychologist, Denver,
Colorado.

For many years Lorraine Kalil was a cocktail waitress. Now she's a bartender. "It's so much easier than waitressing. . . . The most important thing about this job is knowing how to talk to people. You get to know everybody who comes in. The people here tonight are all regulars. . . .

"There is a definite difference between how they treat a man and a woman bartender. Things run better with a woman. Why? It's simple. They won't punch me in the face."

Lorraine Kalil, bartender in Old London Pub at Lenox Hotel, Boston, Massachusetts.

**Wrappers and packers at Liggett and Myers Tobacco
Company, Durham, North Carolina.**

Governor Ella Grasso campaigns in West Hartford, Connecticut.

The young Republican man running against Ella Grasso for governor of Connecticut in 1974 tried to turn her into a joke: "The state can't afford a governess," or "The citizens are too old for a governess" were some of his lead lines. But Ella Grasso started getting elected to public office more than twenty years ago. The sexist jokes didn't get many laughs, and Connecticut became the first state to elect a woman governor who ran on her own merits instead of her husband's coattails.

Journalists breezing into Connecticut to write about "the woman" candidate tried to make her appear to be removed, or different, from the average woman, even the average woman candidate. "Voting for Ella is like voting for a man," they liked to find people saying.

But women were some of Governor Grasso's staunchest supporters. Some members of the South End Democratic Ladies Club of Hartford joined the line of march when Ella campaigned in West Hartford six months before the election. They are the women who have cooked dinners and raised funds and walked streets to raise votes for male candidates. These women don't run for office. "But that's coming," said one of them. "Ella is a good candidate, we'll work hard for her. I've watched her career for many years. You know she even studied political science in college. I always wished I could do what she did. But I didn't have an education." She thinks awhile. "I'm glad she's doing it. Eventually there will be more of us."

Margaret Bodfish, plumber, Orinda, California.

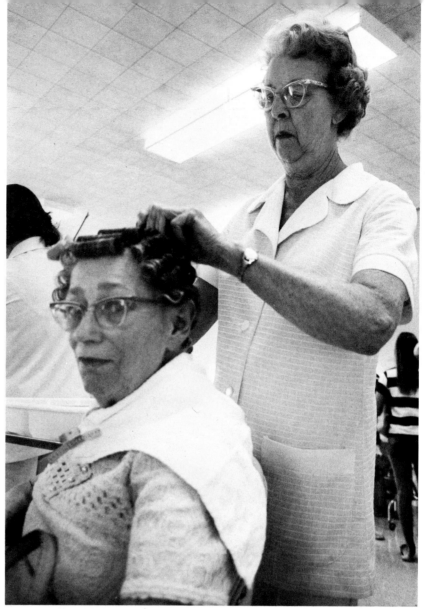
Evelyn Blackman, beautician at Bonnie Lassie Beauty Shop, Menlo Park, California.

"I tried being a waitress, but it only lasted a short time. I can't smile and be pretty. I can't be phony with people. I was not a pretty girl and I could not try to be. I just wanted to do something I liked and be judged for the quality of my work, not on what I looked like. . . . I went back to plumbing. . . . I've owned my own business for three years.

"There was a photographer here taking my picture for a magazine. . . . He kept saying, 'You're going to get yourself dirty.' Well, what's wrong with that? Women are washable, too. Other people say women shouldn't do it because the equipment is dangerous. Well, a Waring blender will cut your finger off if you put your finger in it. People don't say women shouldn't use Waring blenders. All you have to do is understand the equipment."—*Margaret Bodfish.*

Nora Pittman, tow truck operator at Jimmy Carter's
service station, Greensboro, North Carolina.

Janine Stern, vice president of information services division of Programming Methods, a division of General Telephone and Electronics, meeting with her staff.

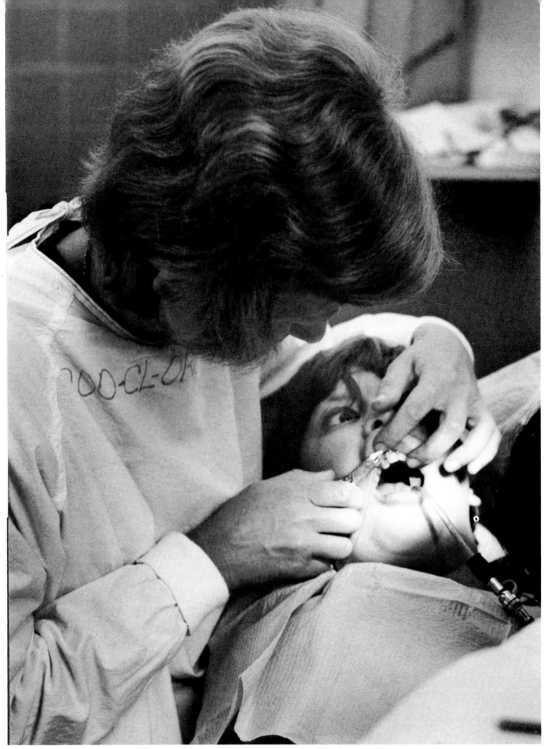

Dr. Karin Vargervik, orthodontist, University of
California Medical Center, San Francisco, California.

"Because dentists can regulate their hours dentistry is a perfect field
for women. But for some reason, in this country the profession has
been much firmer than other branches of medicine in keeping women
out of the schools."—*Dr. Karin Vargervik.*

"It is probably because women have such a hard time getting into
dental schools that we find that many women entering dental hygiene
studies have higher grades than the best men entering dental school."
—*A dental school professor.*

Margaret Collins, fire lookout at Clear Lake Butte
Lookout in Mount Hood National Forest, Maupin,
Oregon.

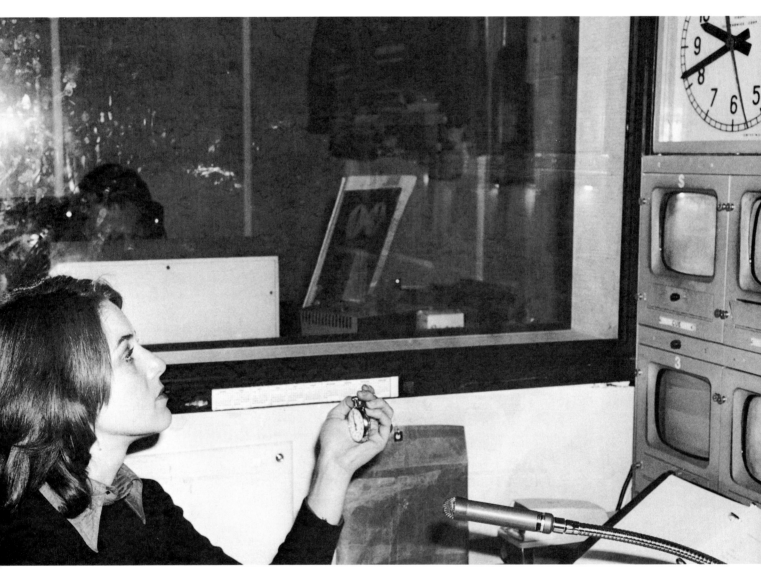

Anne Goodall, assistant director and stage manager, KNXT-TV, Los Angeles, California.

**Mrs. Anna Mangialardo, cashier at Mangialardo &
Sons Italian grocery store, Washington, D.C.**

**Switchboard operators for Chesapeake and Potomac
Telephone Company, Washington, D.C.**

**Barbara Morrison, linewoman with New England
Telephone and Telegraph, Boston, Massachusetts.**

Consuelo Durr, dance teacher, Cambridge, Massachusetts.

106

"Spring comes into Maine like a lovely shy child who makes his appearance with a smile and then darts away again. It never enters brusquely, proclaiming: I'm here to stay. Spring in Maine is almost apologetic to winter, which is downright reluctant to leave. Spring gurgles through the mud, presses down half an inch through the frozen ground, sweeps a warm wind over leafless trees."

—From a letter written by Sister Lucy and two other contemplative Catholic sisters. The three of them live at their Monastery Hermitage in Orland, Maine. Not far from the Hermitage is HOME, a cooperative they helped establish, that sells the art and craft works of about a thousand local residents.

Sister Lucy, sheepherder, Orland, Maine.

Linda Martin, front, tacking belt loops on blue jeans,
and Amelia Zucco, sewing hip pockets on blue jeans
at Trimble's Manufacturing Co. Inc., New Florence,
Pennsylvania.

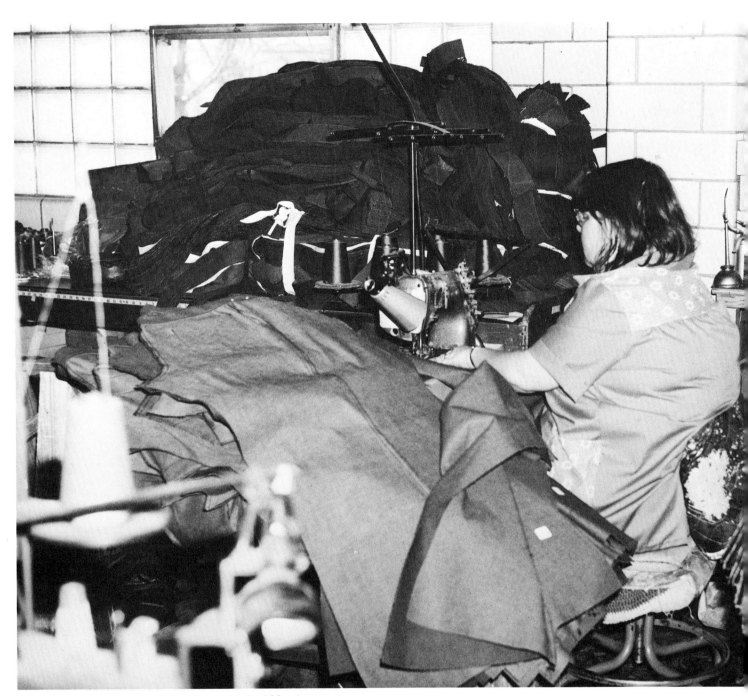

Sudie Barndt, sewing yokes on back of blue jeans, at
Trimble's Manufacturing Co., Inc., New Florence,
Pennsylvania.

"I only know of one other woman, a friend of mine, who does lobstering. I don't know why they don't do it. There's nothing to it. I've been lobstering since I was ten years old. I took ten years leave off the water after I got married at twenty-one. I had a little girl but she died at birth. She'd probably be out here lobstering if she had lived. . . . After ten years I went back on the water. It's like a fever with me.

"You see, I was the daughter of a lighthouse keeper over there on Little Nash Island. There were nine children. It was a great life out there. But, like all things, you don't know it 'til it's past. . . . I own another island now and sometimes camp there five days a week. I keep a couple hundred sheep on the island, but it's not paying anymore. Costs too much to have them sheared. And this spring I lost sixty sheep to the sea gulls. They attack them in droves. . . .

Jenny Cirone, lobsterwoman, South Addison, Maine.

"... I love the lobstering, but it's getting tough, too. I get $1.13 a pound. Most of them aren't big enough and have to be thrown away. Out of twenty-two traps I pulled today, I got only three lobster. . . .

"I'm getting kind of messed up, cysts in my hands and my legs. But I'm gonna stay on the water as long as I can. I guess I'm trying to prove to my husband that I'm not stupid. He hates the water himself."—*Jenny Cirone*.

**Kathleen Fraser, poet, reading her own poetry at
reading at Manhattan Theatre Club, New York City.**

**Barbara Scott, a black belt karate teacher at the
Central YWCA, Washington, D.C.**

Frankie Poe, paperhanger, Pittsboro, North Carolina.

The interview in the *Burlington* (N.C.) *Daily Times-News* quoted Frankie Poe as saying that her male colleagues in the paperhanging business were amused, but "most of them just pick at me and tease me about being a woman's libber."

The reporter apparently thought that a "woman's libber" comes in a single standard model and felt obligated to explain:

"Her work notwithstanding, Frankie neither looks nor acts like a typical 'woman's libber.' An attractive brunette with a low, feminine voice, she dresses in soft sweaters and stylish pants in her work."

They bombed her newspaper office. They financed a new paper to put her out of business. They put her at the top of their list for murder.

This has been the experience of Hazel Brannon Smith, one of the few American publishers and editors to risk their lives for racial justice and for freedom of the press.

As editor and publisher of the *Lexington Advertiser* and other weeklies in Holmes County, Mississippi, for the last thirty years she has spoken out against racism and other injustice. In a time when powerful white men feared to speak against the dominant white supremacists, she minced no words. When a county sheriff, Richard Byrd, shot a black man, she investigated personally, determined the full story, reported it as straight news and then editorialized: "Byrd has violated every concept of justice, decency and right. He is not fit to occupy office."

She won the Pulitzer Prize for her editorials in 1964 and still publishes her papers with the fiery concern for local justice that she had when she bought her first paper in Holmes County in 1935. Back in the 1930s, she wrote an editorial supporting a venereal disease clinic for the poor, against the opposition of the "respectable" folk in town. Her beau of the moment, son of a socially prominent family, chastised her: "Ladies just don't talk about venereal disease." Hazel told him, "I'm no lady. I'm a newspaper woman."

Hazel Brannon Smith, newspaper owner, publisher, editor, reporter, Lexington, Mississippi.

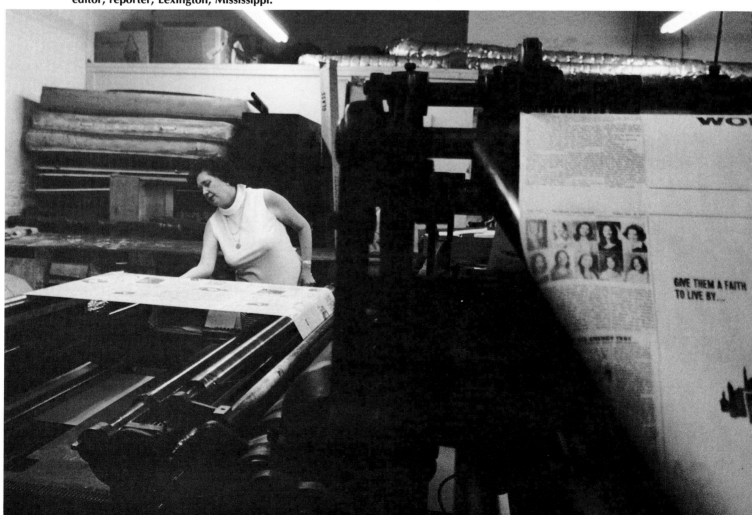

Clorine Stanfield, left, and Martha Graves, sock stretchers, Baker-Cammack Hosiery Mills, Burlington, North Carolina.

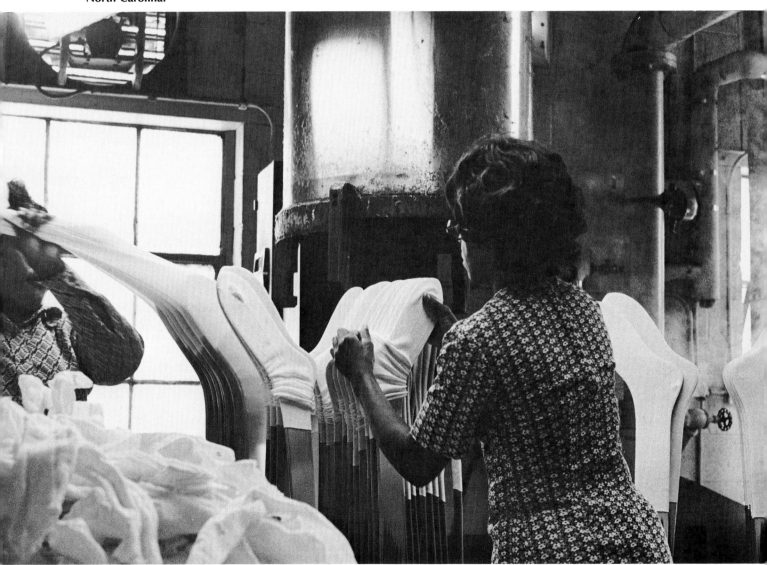

**Dayle Haddon, model at shooting session for
newspaper advertisement, Los Angeles, California.**

"I originally wanted to be a dancer. I did the modeling just to make some money, not because I really wanted to do it. Now I want to be an actress and I still do the modeling to make money. I just completed an Italian film. . . .

"Modeling is really an insult to your intelligence. There's no challenge, no creativity in it. . . . I hate the clothes I wear when I model. I'd never wear them as my own.

"I usually wear blue jeans and a T-shirt and things I can pick up at the Paris flea market. The clothes this year are particularly appalling. A photographer who recently shot me for *Elle* had me chew cookies as he shot me. It was his way of making fun of the clothes. . . ."—*Dayle Haddon.*

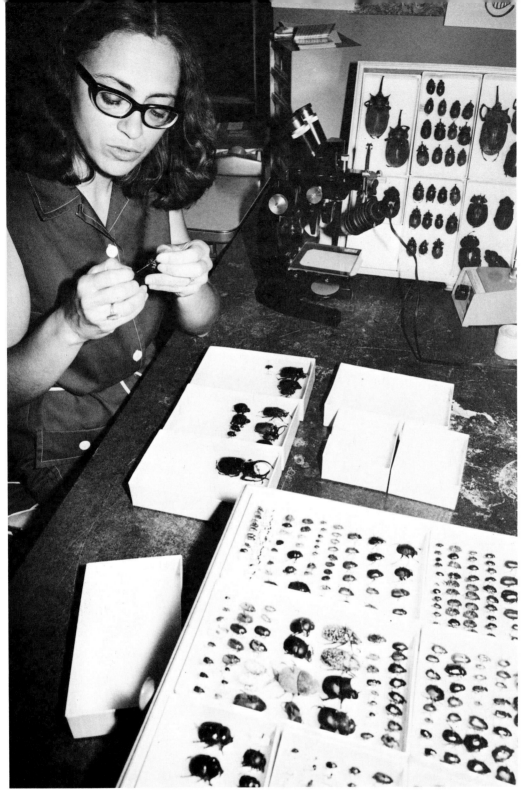

Janice C Scott, curatorial associate in insect
collection at Museum of Comparative Zoology of
Harvard University, Cambridge, Massachusetts.

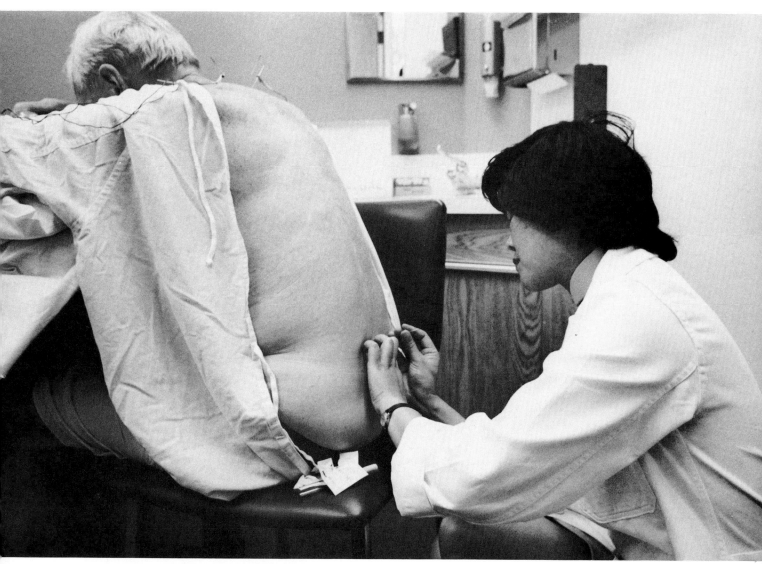

Margaret Tan, acupuncturist at University of
California Medical Center, San Francisco, California.

Like a number of other senior citizens in Upshur County in West Virginia, Ora Kincaid comes regularly to the basement of the Community Action Program in Buckhannon to use the lapidary equipment. She was carefully refining a rough piece of red glass one day in March 1974. She asked me to guess what it had been. I didn't know. "It was the taillight of a '67 Dodge. They were real nice. Can't get them anymore. They're all plastic now. That was the last year the Dodge had glass taillights." In its second life the extinct taillight is a delicately crafted pin and tie tack.

Ora Kincaid, jewelry maker, Buckhannon, West Virginia.

**Patricia Allen, computer operator for American
Security Bank, Washington, D.C.**

"I don't know why the bank didn't have any women in this job before.
I've come up through the ranks. I used to be a teller and also was on
keypunch. I wanted to do this. There is no reason why a woman
shouldn't be able to do it. There isn't even anything physically difficult
about it. Lifting those boxes of paper is the most strenuous thing I do.
Actually, most days the men lift those boxes. But on the days when I
wear short skirts, they make me lift the boxes."—*Patricia Allen.*

**Peggy Sullivan, African area supervisor at the
Louisville, Kentucky, Zoo, with giraffes Milhous,
Tricia and Julie.**

Wendy Aberdeen, hansom carriage driver in Central Park, New York City.

Air Force Lt. Una D. Hampton, going to work several stories underground at missile site near Topeka, Kansas.

Air Force Lt. Una (Cissy) D. Hampton works in the deep, underground control rooms of the United States missile sites in rural Kansas. A graduate of college and of Officers Candidate School, she wants to make a career of the Air Force. "I wanted in because I always thought it would be a nice life. I like it mainly because of the money. I now make $600 a month, plus $100 for rooming. That's twice as much money as my brother makes."

In 1960 Richard Nixon, vice president of the
United States, was at Notre Dame University
receiving the student body's annual
Americanism Award. A Catholic monsignor was
seated across from the vice president's wife, Pat
Nixon.

"As her dinner partner, it was difficult to keep
the conversation moving," he recalls. "So, I
said, 'Do you find the life of being the wife of a
politician intellectually attractive and
stimulating? If you do, being the wife of the vice
president must be a marvelous experience. If
you don't, I suppose it's burdensome."

He remembers that she waited what seemed a
very long time. Then she leaned across the table
and said:

"I have sacrificed everything in my life that I
consider precious in order to advance the
political career of my husband."

Thelma Ryan ("Pat") Nixon, long-time campaign worker/wife of former President Richard Nixon, greeting guests May 13, 1974, at the annual "Senate Ladies Luncheon" at the White House.

Irene Mejia, urging a boycott of nonunion wine
outside liquor store in Santa Maria, California.

"She pickets and boycotts because of what has happened to her. She and
her family worked in the fields all their lives. She gave birth to some of
her children under bridges and out in the fields. Altogether, she bore
twenty-four children. . . . Irene is very important to the workers here.
Sometimes she comes after the men and forces them to go out to the
picket line. She is a great example to all of us."—*Margarita Flores*,
director of the service center of the United Farm Workers in Santa
Maria, Calif.

Mary Scoblick, partner with her husband, Tony
Scoblick, in the M & T Moving Company, Baltimore,
Maryland.

Trudy Strong, trapeze artist with circus at Capital Centre, Landover, Maryland.

Gertrude Kerbis, architect, in front of building she
designed, the Seven Continents Building at O'Hare
International Airport, Chicago, Illinois.

Gertrude Lemp Kerbis is one of the ten women who ever have been
named fellows of the American Institute of Architects. When she went
to architecture school in the 1940s there was only one other woman in
the class. "It was hell for women architects then. They didn't want us
in school or in the profession. . . . One thing I've never understood
about this prejudice is that it's so strange in view of the fact that the
drive to build has always been in women."

Marie-Luise Flor, wood carver, Rock Cave,
West Virginia.

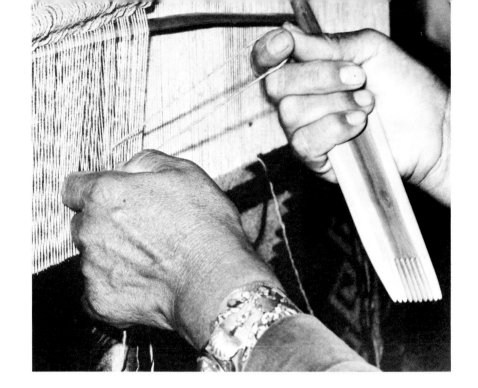

Linda G. Chrisp, compressive shrinkage frame
operator at Burlington House, drapery manufacturing
division of Burlington Industries, Burlington, North
Carolina.

Elsie Wilson, Navajo Indian weaver, Windowrock, Arizona.

Grace Sullivan, tour guide at the Vanderbilt home,
the Breakers, in Newport, Rhode Island.

Berkeley Woman's Music Collective—Debbie, Nancy,
Susann, and Nancy—rehearsing in Berkeley,
California.

"I had been working in the mail room in the office of a big oil company in Houston. I knew I didn't want to keep doing that. I came back to El Paso. . . . My mother talked about how well the engineers did, what nice big cars they drove. . . . My whole family had been railroaders, so I thought I'd try it. . . .

"I'm doing more for myself now than if I had gone to college and got a degree. I can make $1,700 a month. . . . The men have been good about having a woman engineer. Sometimes they'll say, 'I'll help you with that.' I'll say, 'Well, if you want to, but I can do it.' They tease me 'til I don't think I can't be teased anymore."—*Christene Gonzales*.

**Christene Gonzales, engineer for the Santa Fe
Railway Company, working out of El Paso, Texas.**

Sharon Clancy, account executive in Dialog Division
of J. Walter Thompson Advertising and Public
Relations Agency, New York, surrounded by People
Pails, product of one of her clients, Spiegel Industries
Corporation.

Catherine Fricke, raw wool packer at Bartlett Yarns, Inc., Harmony, Maine.

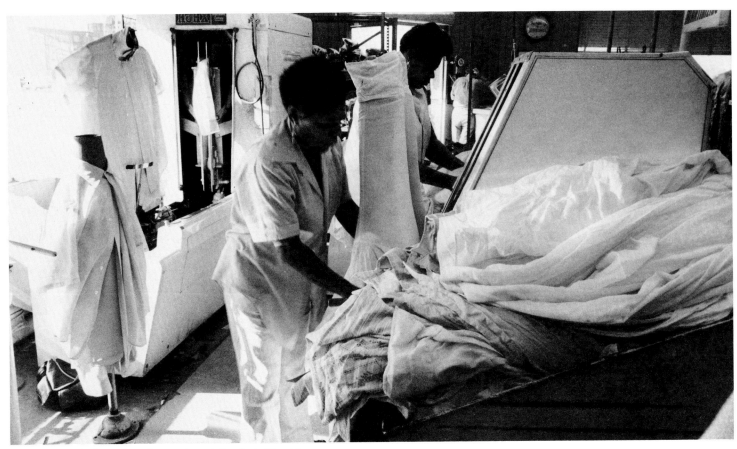

Marie Pace, laundry worker at Kessler's One-Hour
Dry Cleaning, Silver Spring, Maryland.

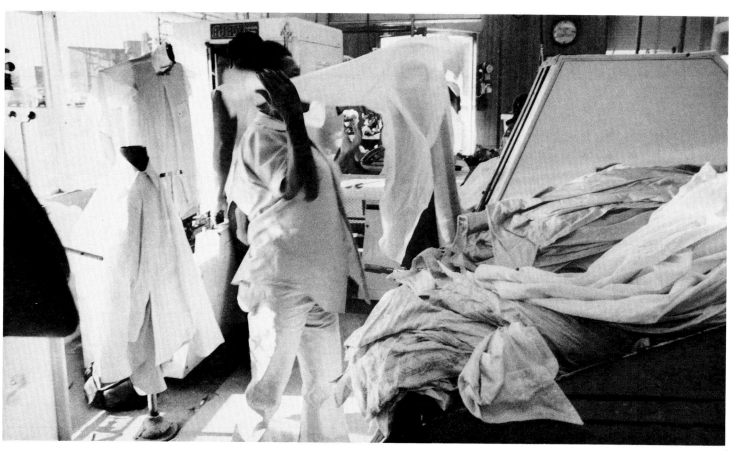

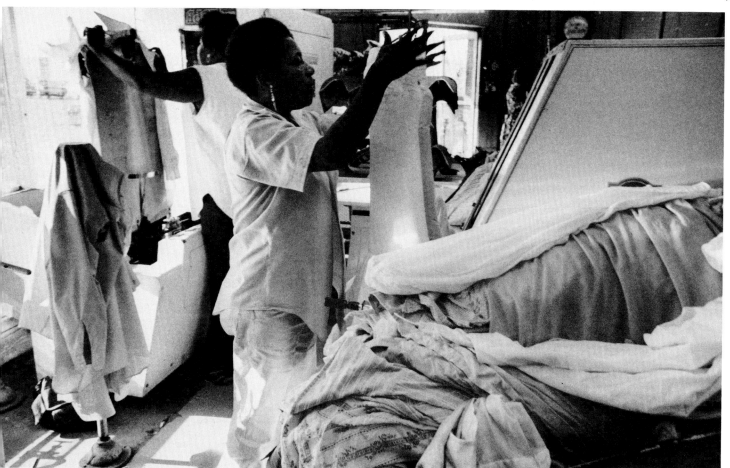

"Ten years ago Everett and I were out here working one day and he slowed down, said he was hard of breath. I said, 'There's something wrong.' He said he'd be okay. But I made him go to a doctor. They said it was just in time. His heart was so large it would've been the end had he not got there. . . . So, I did most of the harvesting since then. Everett goes out and can drive the combine, but he has to be real careful. . . .

"We'd just started building the house a few months before his heart attack. Everett had said, 'Before we die I want us to have a new house.' Well, it looked for a while like Everett wasn't going to live to see the new house.

"That made me start to think. I told Everett I was going to go take the state course to be a nurse's aide. He said, 'What are you doing that for?' Well, I was afraid he'd die and I'd need something else to do. I enjoy this farm work, but it's hard work and I wouldn't want to do it for anybody but Everett. I need something else to do if Everett dies.

"So, in six months I graduated and started working at the hospital in Wellington. I went on with the understanding that I'd have to take off during plowing, planting and harvest seasons. That's how we do it every year. Last year we made $70,000 from the wheat before taxes."—*Estelle Rose*.

Estelle Rose, wheat farmer, Wellington, Kansas.

In 1967, when Patricia Joy already was in her mid-twenties, she said she wanted to grow up to be a television reporter. In the meantime, for about four years she worked as a secretary in the film editing room of a television station. She left the typing to someone else and "tried to learn as much as I could and become valuable in the film room." Then she became a reporter in 1971 and did that until she became a camerawoman in 1973. "I've found that I really like the technical end of the business, that's where my strongest ability is. Besides, with the camera I have more control over the final product." And, people don't call about the camerawoman, as they did about the reporter, and say, "Tell Patricia Joy to cut her hair" or "stop wearing pants" or "change her voice."

Patricia Joy, camerawoman and film editor at KGW-TV, Portland, Oregon.

Marjorie Bolton, assistant baker at Buttercup Bakery,
Oakland, California.

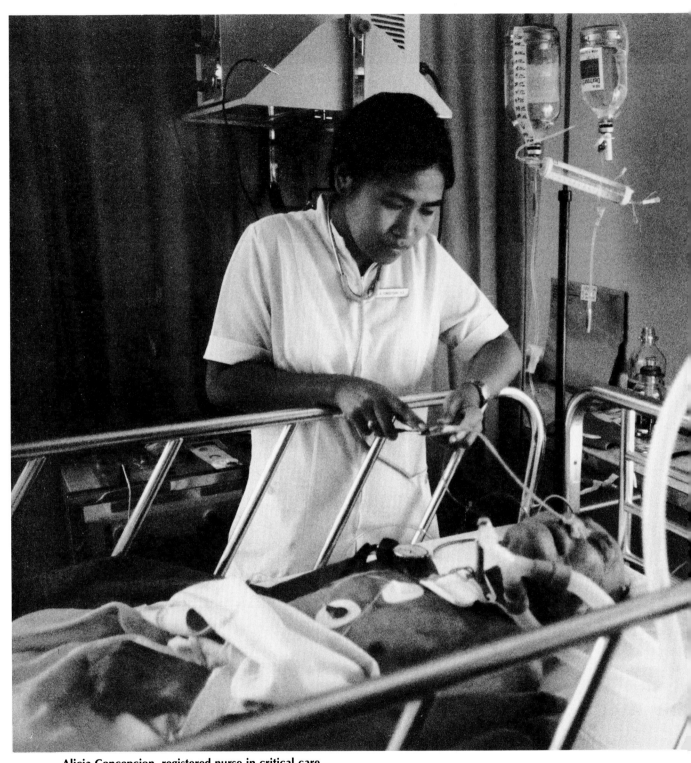

Alicia Concepcion, registered nurse in critical care
unit of Long Beach Community Hospital, Long Beach,
California.

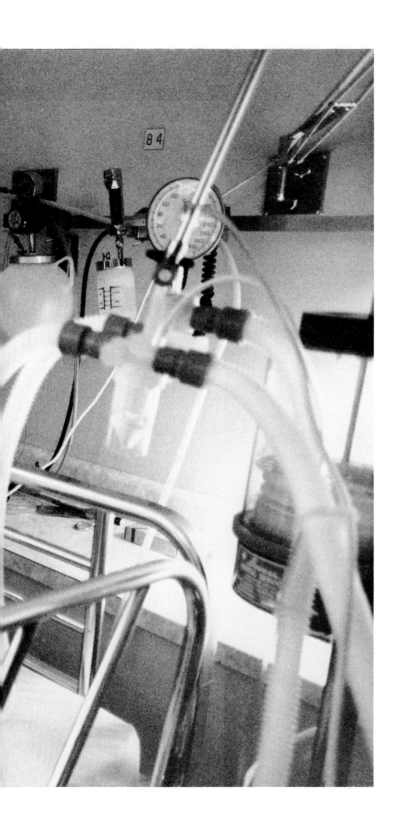

Jeanne Carlysle, courier for WTOP-TV, Washington, D.C.

"I've been a courier in Washington for about thirty years. My mother didn't care too much for it at first. She didn't think it was very feminine. But she got used to it. I do it because I like it—I like riding and I like being outside. Thirty years ago people thought it was a little strange to see a girl riding around town on a bike."—*Jeanne Carlysle*.

Muriel Siebert, stockbroker and member of the New York Stock Exchange, New York City.

"I know a twenty-eight-year-old woman, a recent graduate of Harvard Business School. She asked me the other day if I wasn't afraid of what people will say if I associate with the women's movement. What she doesn't understand is that it's because of the movement and people like me that it's now not as difficult for her to make it."—*Muriel Siebert.*

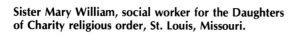
Sister Mary William, social worker for the Daughters of Charity religious order, St. Louis, Missouri.

156

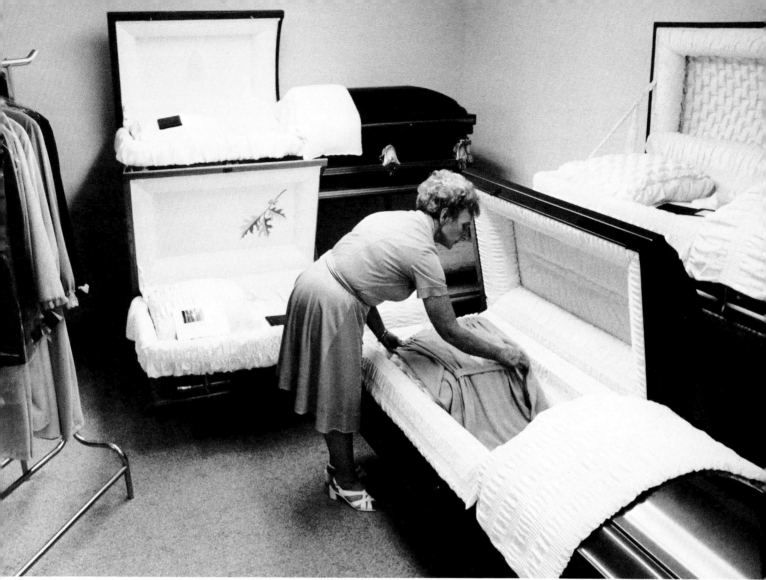

Sue Cusimano, funeral director at Colonial Mortuary,
Mountain View, California.

"I have to fight to prove myself in this business. When people come into
a funeral home they don't expect to deal with a woman. Would you? So,
I have to be especially good to them and prove myself. I'm very nice
about it. . . .

"By the way, are you using color film?" she asked as she draped the
dress inside the green casket. "No," I said, and she sighed, "Good." I
asked why she was concerned. "This is a lavender dress, and I'd never
put a lavender dress in a green casket."

Joan H. Wilson, welder at the Baltimore Plant of
General Motors Assembly Division, Baltimore,
Maryland.

"I like the job. It hasn't begun to be boring yet. Some people tell me it will. I worked
in a nursing home as a nurse's aide before and made $54 a week. Now I make $214 a
week." There's a soft, satisfied laugh.

"I was on the welfare before because I didn't make enough at the job. In the food
stores when I'd take my food stamps out, the people behind me would say things to
each other, such as, 'I bet she lives in a fabulous home.' They'd say it loud enough
for me to hear, and they'd give me dirty looks.

"I always said to myself, 'Ms. Wilson is going to get off the welfare someday and not
go through this.' I was not ashamed, but people would make you feel ashamed. . . . I
worked at the nursing home from eleven at night to seven in the morning. Then I had
to go to school at eight o'clock. It was just a brush up on your elementary education,
and you had to do it or they'd cut part of your check.

"Now, now I feel more independent. I feel like I'm going someplace. I can get the
bills paid, keep the life insurance up to date. My children and I are dressing better.
The four of them and I are moving to a better apartment in a few weeks."—*Joan
Wilson.*

Louise and Louie run Louie's Gulf Station in Rockland, Maine, from seven A.M. to seven P.M. every day. Louise didn't exactly want to work in the gas station or any other place outside her home. In fact, she told Louie she'd go under one condition: that he would put a television set in the station so she could watch the soap operas. He did. She thinks it's worked out pretty well. Louis does the mechanical work, and she pumps all the gas and checks the oil. "I tried having men work for me," said Louie, "but I found them too undependable, and they stole too much. So, I got rid of them and replaced them with her. . . . I'm real proud of her. She does a good job."

Louise Lanphier, gas station attendant, Rockland, Maine.

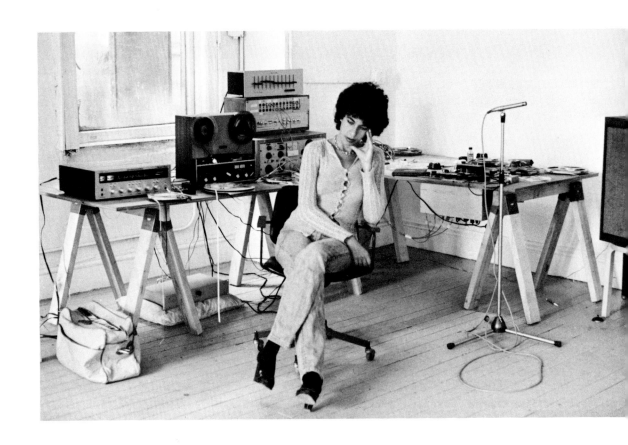

Susan Ain, composer, New York City.

Margarita Flores, service center director of the United Farm Workers union in Santa Maria, California.

Kate Thornhill, a head stevedore on the Miami River, Miami, Florida.

Kate Thornhill was a concert pianist and an educator. She also once was the manager of a wholesale reptile firm and the manager of an aircraft parts company. But to the longshoremen along the Miami River, she is "Tugboat Kate," perhaps the only woman in the world who is a head stevedore.

Mrs. Thornhill got into the shipping business after a tragedy in 1956, when she was already in her fifties. She slipped on a tile floor and shattered a leg and critically injured her back. Told that she'd never walk again, she decided to start her own shipping business while still in a Miami hospital. With one leg in traction, a phone at her side and a typewriter suspended over her bed, she managed to net $10,000 profit by the time she left the hospital six months later. Within a few years she operated and owned three successful businesses—a stevedoring operation, the shipping company, and an aircraft parts firm.

Kiane Nowell, a lifeguard on the Venice Beach, Los
Angeles, California.

"Not a day goes by that somebody doesn't say, 'Are you really a lifeguard? If you are, I'm going to go out and drown.'"—*Kiane Nowell*, the only woman guard on the ocean beaches in Los Angeles County.

Lt. Sally D. Murphy, helicopter pilot in military intelligence, Fort Rucker, Alabama.

"I was up in Washington last week doing some work on service bills for the Army and Senator Goldwater. You know, the Army has this real bad image because of the Vietnam war. They think we're killers. So, the Army sent me up to help promote some Armed Service bills because of their bad image. It helps, I guess, to put women out front.

". . . After they let me progress at the same rate as the other students, my training went very well. It was a strong pressure knowing that if you washed out, you might make it impossible for other women after you. . . .

"I'll be learning fixed wing craft next. . . . I'll probably be assigned to electronic warfare—err, I should say electronic surveillance. Everybody gets all upset about the word 'warfare.'"—*Army Lt. Sally Murphy*.

**Dr. Candace Oviatt, oceanographer at University of
Rhode Island, Kingston, Rhode Island.**

Norma Mann, president of Mann Steel Company,
Dallas, Texas.

Norma Mann was a payroll clerk in a reinforcing steel company until seventeen years ago when her boss died and she was assigned by a judge to complete his contracts. Since then she has become president of Mann Steel Co., Inc., the largest single employer of iron workers in the Southwest. Her annual volume has been more than $1 million for the past six years.

Nearly every major new building on the Dallas skyline has been reinforced with steel from Mann.

"There have been problems because of my being a woman. There was one general contractor who refused to deal with me in the early years. He would say, 'I know Norma Mann is good, but I'm not going to deal with a woman.' I had tried and tried to deal with him at first and then decided, okay, if that's the way he is, let him be.

"Two years later he called me one day and said, 'Norma, I've got this job I'd like you to bid on.' I said, 'Why, sure.' We've done almost all his work since that day. Our reputation was so strong and good that there came a time when he had to deal with me. . . . Because I'm a woman I had to be better than anybody else.

"People will ask my men how they feel about working for a woman. They'll say, 'I don't work for a woman. I work for Norma.' I haven't figured out yet whether that's an insult or a compliment."
—*Norma Mann.*

**Bernice O. Pearley, sweeping in cutting department
of Liggett and Myers Tobacco Company, Durham,
North Carolina.**

**Cheerleaders for Redskins professional football team,
Washington, D.C.**

"Archeology has not had much of a problem accepting women. That's probably because there has always been room in archeology for the eccentrics."—*Cordelia Snow.*

Cordelia Thomas Snow, archeologist excavating Governor's Palace, Santa Fe, New Mexico.

Myra Kressner, director of Play Group, a day-care
center in New York City.

**Brenda Adam, air traffic controller, Air Route Traffic
Control Center, Aurora, Illinois.**

"I used to be a secretary in a bank. I wanted to work my way up, but
they made it clear a woman would never work her way up in that
bank." So, Brenda Adam now sits in front of a radar screen in the
cavernous Air Route Traffic Control Center in Aurora, Ill., and helps
control air traffic in the upper third of the Midwest.

It is legend that the tension is so great at such centers that controllers
have been known to commit suicide after a large plane crash in their
territory. After redirecting one pilot off a collision course, Brenda
casually talks about why she likes her tension-filled job. "This is so
much better than being a secretary. I have responsibility, and I like
that. I have to be confident or the pilots won't have anything to do
with my instructions. They have to know I know what I'm doing."

Barbara James, assembly technician building
electronic modules for jet aircraft at Rudolph
Precision Assemblies, Inc., Kansas City, Missouri.

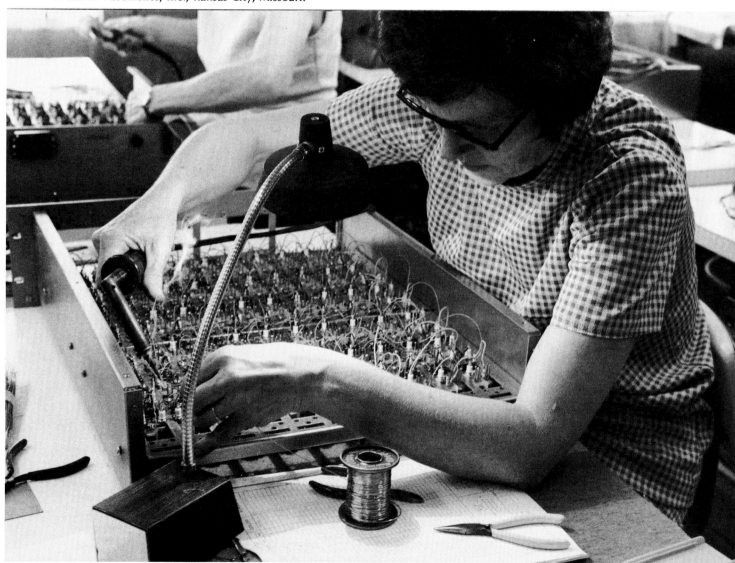

Sherry Suttles, assistant city manager, Menlo Park, California.

"I'm in city management because I see it as a way of trying to cause change at the grassroots level. At the moment, I'm a little overwhelmed by the lack of power of the manager and at how City Council controls him. . . . There are very few women in the field, partly because of the old boy network. Many of them graduated from the same places and know each other and get each other jobs."
—*Sherry Suttles*.

"I was a beautician. I got to know everything fast. Then I was bored. When you're a hairdresser, you talk about the same things, do the same hair styles. You don't have a chance to grow. I didn't like it after a while.

"One day I made a list of my good points and my bad points. I figured that somehow I'd have to get into the selling profession. But what? I knew I didn't want to sell hosiery. I'd always been a car nut, so I thought, why not? I like getting up in the morning now. That's pretty good when you consider that 90 percent of the people hate going to work.

"The first couple of months I was scared to death. You would not believe the amount of technical knowledge, all about the engine, you have to know. . . . Here I'm dealing one hour with a factory worker, the next with the president of a multimillion dollar corporation. I have to talk to both of them on their levels, get into their backgrounds. . . . They have to have a lot of confidence in me if they're going to invest that much money. That's a good feeling."—*Nada Ray*.

Nada C. Ray, car saleswoman, Cass Ford, Des Plaines, Illinois.

Barbara Taggart, left, and Evelyn Persoff, mechanics
at the Cooperative Garage, Watertown,
Massachusetts.

Evelyn Persoff was a fine arts major in college and later worked
with puppet theater groups. She thinks her art studies helped
prepare her hands for the dexterity she now uses on Volkswagen
engines.

Barbara Taggart, a former high school French teacher, didn't find
teaching French very interesting. In the meantime, she learned how
to fix her own car, liked doing so, and decided to drop French for
fixing cars full time.

**Patricia Cook, flagwoman at Metro subway
construction site, Washington, D.C.**

Judge Elreta Melton Alexander, in the General Court
of Justice, Greensboro, North Carolina.

"Being a woman judge was, of course, a great shock. Being competent made it
an even greater shock. But I think being a woman has been an advantage.

". . . I don't think in terms of male and female, except for the biblical mandate
to be fruitful and multiply. I understand that in the brain there are two sides—
the left is the reasoning, or pragmatic side, the right is the inspirational side.
Society has trained us to think that only one of those sides is developed in each
sex—the reasoning side in man, the inspirational or emotional in women.

"But if you throw off the psychosis of the society and get it all together—
develop both sides of the brain—you can do anything. . . . That's part of the
liberation of humanity."—*Judge Elreta Melton Alexander.*

Virginia Harmon, front, and other women making
apple butter for the Brucetown Methodist Church,
Brucetown, Virginia.

Lea Jane Berinati developed a long-range plan for her career at age sixteen. She wanted to be a singer. The route, she figured then, should begin with majoring in music in college, and then working for five years as a secretary in Nashville. Secretary for five years?

"I thought the only way I could succeed would be if I knew the business thoroughly. And that the only way I could get to know the business thoroughly was by moving from one department to another as a secretary." For five years after college she did exactly that at Columbia studios. Eventually, she started sticking around the studio evenings and picked up jobs as a singer, pianist or drummer when extras were needed for recording sessions.

"All of which led to her now being the only woman recording engineer in Nashville, the recording capital. She still fills in when a group needs an extra for a recording session. That's for fun. Professionally she is concentrating on the engineering.

Lea Jane Berinati, recording engineer at Mercury Studios, Nashville, Tennessee.

**Dorothea Hammond, left, actress, and Zelda
Fichandler, producing director, Arena Stage,
Washington, D.C.**

Alice Hector, lawyer, with client at Bernalillo County Jail, Albuquerque, New Mexico.

"I think the hardest thing for a woman lawyer is to develop a style in the courtroom. There are no role models for women lawyers. The male role models are offensive to your average juror if a woman adopts them. . . .

"But I feel a woman has an advantage in one way. Male lawyers are so caught up in the machismo thing. Often when they deal with the prosecutor it's a matter of which one of them is going to win, and the interests of the client are far in the background. It's more a matter of which one is going to come off as super lawyer. I'm not playing that game. I go to the D.A. and I talk about the client, talk about what's really going to be best for that person. Unlike the lawyer with the machismo, I don't mind begging over and over for my client."—*Alice Hector.*

REFERENCE

**Ruth Fondi, director of Sewickley Public Library,
Sewickley, Pennsylvania.**

Kathleen Marpe, coach and physical education instructor, University of New Mexico, Albuquerque, New Mexico.

"The whole idea of equality of women has made a big difference in sports. We've got a long way to go. We're just now starting, and only at a couple schools, to give even small scholarships for women athletes. . . .

"I just graduated in 1971. When I went out for sports you were called a jock, unfeminine. The only people who watched your games were other athletes. Even my parents didn't want me to go out. They thought I'd injure myself so I wouldn't be able to have babies and be a good wife. . . ."—*Kathy Marpe.*

"This rig is a good one. They let me do everything. All I want out of a job is steady work and a chance to do everything there is to do. On some jobs they wouldn't let me do much. They'd say, 'You'll need help with that.' These guys let me work. I feel if I can't do the work I shouldn't be here. . . . When my husband and I married he worked on a rig at night. I'd drive him to work and sit in the car all night watching the work. I loved to watch it. Then I started to think: if I like this so much I might as well do it myself. . . . My husband hates me for doing it."—*Jackie Lacouture*.

**Jackie Lacouture, roughneck on the night shift on an
oil rig in Lockport, Louisiana.**

**Republican State Representative Susan Catania in the
state house, Springfield, Illinois.**

Over one arm Illinois State Representative Susan Catania carries a canvas bag that has feminist Susan B. Anthony's name and portrait emblazoned on it. Half of the bag contains correspondence from her constituents. The other half is filled with diapers. That's because on her other arm, as she walks to the state assembly chambers in Springfield, Ill., is Amy, the fifth of her children. Amy spent a good portion of the first six months of her life in the chambers.

Amy would sleep or play peacefully in a car bed beside her mother in the assembly chambers. When nursing time came, Rep. Catania and Amy went to the nearest restroom. By the time they returned to the chambers they had spent less time outside the chambers than the average legislator who left the floor to consult with aides or lobbyists.

Though photographers are ordinarily permitted inside the chambers, they wouldn't allow me to take pictures on the floor of Mrs. Catania with her baby. They even kicked me out of the public gallery.As we talked in the hall outside the chambers, Rep. Catania's seatmate, another representative, strolled by. Introduced to me, he said, "Why don't you go take pictures of my wife? She does something unusual: she stays home and takes care of our home and children. . . . It's so nice having Mrs. Catania as a seatmate. She adds considerable excitement to the environment by her presence. It's certainly better scenery than sitting next to a man."

Mary Jane Walters, printer with KNOW, a feminist publishing collective, Pittsburgh, Pennsylvania.

"This is hard work. Frankly, I don't think many men could do it. It requires a great amount of patience they don't have. People are always breaking appointments, changing their minds. Men can't stand that. That's why women are taking over real estate. I don't think the women's lib people could do it either. They aren't patient."—*Rosamond Walling Tirana*.

Rosamond Walling Tirana, real estate agent, Washington, D.C.

Patricia B. Franzen, production foreman trainee at
Pittsburgh Works of Jones and Laughlin Steel
Corporation, Pittsburgh, Pennsylvania.

"I came in as a laborer just for the summer. I had been teaching high school physics and chemistry. I took the summer job because we needed the money. . . . By early August they asked me to come on full time as a trainee foreman. For someone as interested in chemistry and physics and geology as I was, it was a hard thing to pass up; the mill is like a lab. But I could not decide right away. When you are the sole support of two kids you want to be pretty secure. I was very secure in my teaching job; I'd been there for three years and had control of it.

"But I decided that I don't need security as long as I have courage. . . . I feel now that as long as there's soap and water I want to stay in the steel mill. . . . I came home the other night with graphite on my face. I was black and glistening. My little girl said, 'When you get washed, Mommy, you'll still be pretty.' My kids loved shopping with me for my steel-toed shoes. What other mommy wears things like that and brings home a piece of coke?

"I'm learning more here than I did studying for my master's degree. I ask questions all the time, and the men answer in great detail. . . . When I was a laborer I asked some of the men what they thought of my becoming a boss. The best advice was: 'Sure, but don't act like you know more than you do. And ask questions.'

"One of the nicest things is that I'm accepted as me at the mill. I put my hair in a top knot under a hard hat, put on mascara so you can tell I have eyes, put on jeans and a shirt and feel comfortable. They accept me as a person, not as a female trying to compete with them. . . . When I was teaching, I spent a lot of money on graduate courses and on my family. I didn't have money for expensive clothes. But most of the other women were their family's second income. They spent a lot of money on hair, make-up and clothes. I didn't like that. . . . But the biggest difference between teaching and working in the mill is that there's room for my mind to expand at the mill; there wasn't any more room for that where I taught."—*Patty Franzen.*

Diane De Blasio, water meter repairer for the water department of Vancouver City, Washington.

Anne Halfen, breaking out beef hindquarters at King
Foods, St. Paul, Minnesota.

Dr. Mary Gray, professor of mathematics, American
University, Washington, D.C.

During her first year in graduate school at the University of Kansas, Dr. Mary Gray complained to a professor about how he had graded her exam. He answered that it didn't matter "because you're just going to stay home and take care of kids."

And the dean of her graduate school, shortly before she got her Ph.D. in mathematics, said, "Women don't get degrees in math because they aren't that kind of people."

Nevertheless, she is a full professor in mathematics at American University. One of her concerns is getting teachers to stop encouraging a fear of mathematics, particularly among girls. "Because they don't like it themselves, many elementary teachers make girls afraid of it. They make them think it's a special treat to skip a day of math."

Sally Priesand is the first woman rabbi in the history of Judaism. "I think they accepted me at rabbinical school because they thought I came to get a husband. Many people didn't really believe I would become a rabbi.

". . .It never seemed unusual to me. I didn't even think about being 'the first' until I started getting all the publicity. What I was doing seemed very natural to me. I suppose that was partly because my parents were so supportive. They didn't say, 'Why's a nice Jewish girl like you becoming a rabbi?' . . . I think it's been much more difficult for women in the congregation than for men. Clergy are father figures to many women, and sometimes they are threatened by another woman accomplishing what they see as strictly male goals. But I can see them replacing that feeling with a sense of pride that women can have that role."

Rabbi Sally Priesand of Stephen Wise Free Synagogue, New York City.

200

Florence Harnden, chairperson of the Muckleshoot
Tribe, Auburn, Washington.

"My dad was on the tribal council. Granddad was a chief. A lot of people call
me the chief. I've been the chairperson of the council for six years. Even as a
young woman I wanted to be a leader of my people. . . .

"I figure what any man can do, any woman can do. . . . Sometimes I'm out
patrolling the fishing all night long. Some of the fishermen call me dirty names,
and I swear right back at them. You have to. It's the only way they listen. . . .

"Let me show you something. See all those trailers? That's right in the middle
of our tribe's property, all those trailers right up against each other. Some white
man—excuse me—came in one night and got the Indian woman who owned it
drunk and then had her sign papers. She didn't know until weeks later, when he
came to evict her, that she had sold the property. . . . Our people have many
needs, people do them in too often. But I can't be the leader much longer; it
takes everything out of you. In addition to being their leader, some of them see
me as a mother figure. I have to do all the cooking for ceremonial events—that's
for four or five hundred people. They call at all hours of the night for help with
sick problems, family problems, or help with the welfare. And I'm sick about
what the drugs are doing to our young people."—*Florence "Dossie" Harnden.*

Rita Kay Cox, truck driver for Industrial Asphalt,
Santa Fe Springs, California.

"I never thought anything about discrimination 'til I started trying to get hired as a trucker. I'd go in looking for a job and they'd say they had no secretarial openings. I'd say, 'That's not what I'm here for.' They'd say, 'What do you do?' I'd tell them I was a trucker. Then there'd be a horse laugh and they'd make a lot of smart remarks to each other. . . .

"It's hard when you meet guys socially. When they find out I'm a trucker, they say, 'Oh, a women's libber,' and walk away. I'm hurt by that. I'm not trying to compare with any man. . . . So I got that I'd not tell anybody what I did until after they knew me pretty well. Instead, I'd lie and tell them I was a meat wrapper—which I used to be—or a secretary or a hair stylist. As you can see, I think it's pretty important to be feminine. I don't want guys thinking I'm a butch. . . .

"I think the women's liberation movement probably has affected me, too. Some nights I work twelve hours and don't get home 'til 5 A.M. And then a few hours later my boyfriend might come in and ask me to fix him a sandwich. Now I tell him: 'Look, I'm not trying to compare with you, but I worked twelve hours last night and I'm tired. You have two hands, make your own sandwich.'"—*Rita Cox*, age nineteen, mother of a four-year-old son, separated from her husband.

"I never had any contact with black people until I started working for Head Start in Holmes County in 1969. In fact, I was one of the leading citizens who campaigned for private schools. I didn't want my children to go to integrated schools. . . . Then I got to know black people. . . . And I saw children who had never eaten off plates, never seen themselves in a mirror, and children and adults who had never seen a medical person. . . . They changed me. . . . I realized that even Head Start was too late. That's why I went into midwifery. . . . We've seen the county's infant mortality rate go down about 50 percent since the midwife program started in 1970. Last year the four of us delivered 78 percent of all babies born in the county. . . .

"I never know when I help bring a baby out what kind of great person I have in my hands, maybe an opera singer. That's a wonderful moment. It's good being in on the beginning instead of the end."

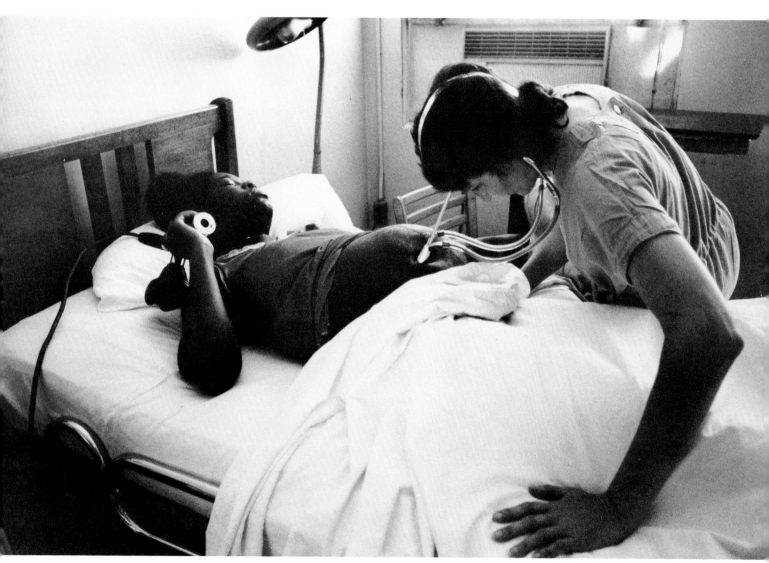

Nancy Umphers, nurse-midwife, examines Irene Epps
at Holmes County Community Hospital, Lexington,
Mississippi.

"Hey, Irene, we got us a beautiful baby!"—*midwife Nancy Umphers* to Irene Epps, the new mother.

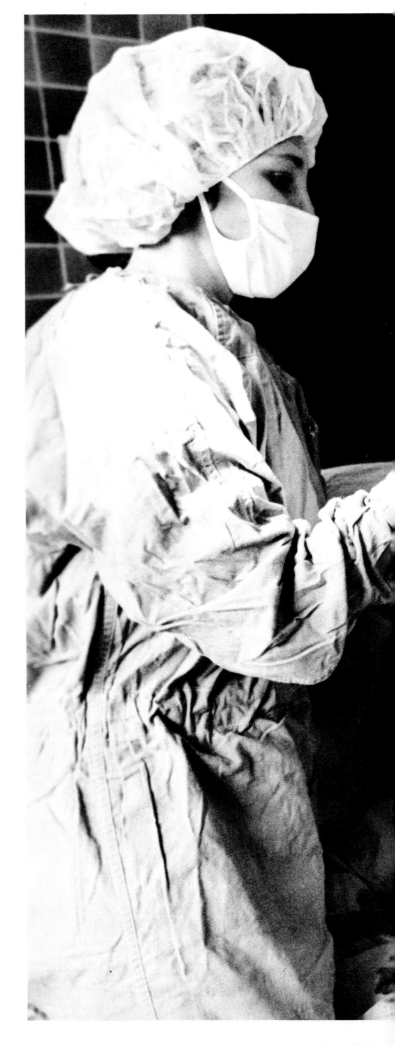

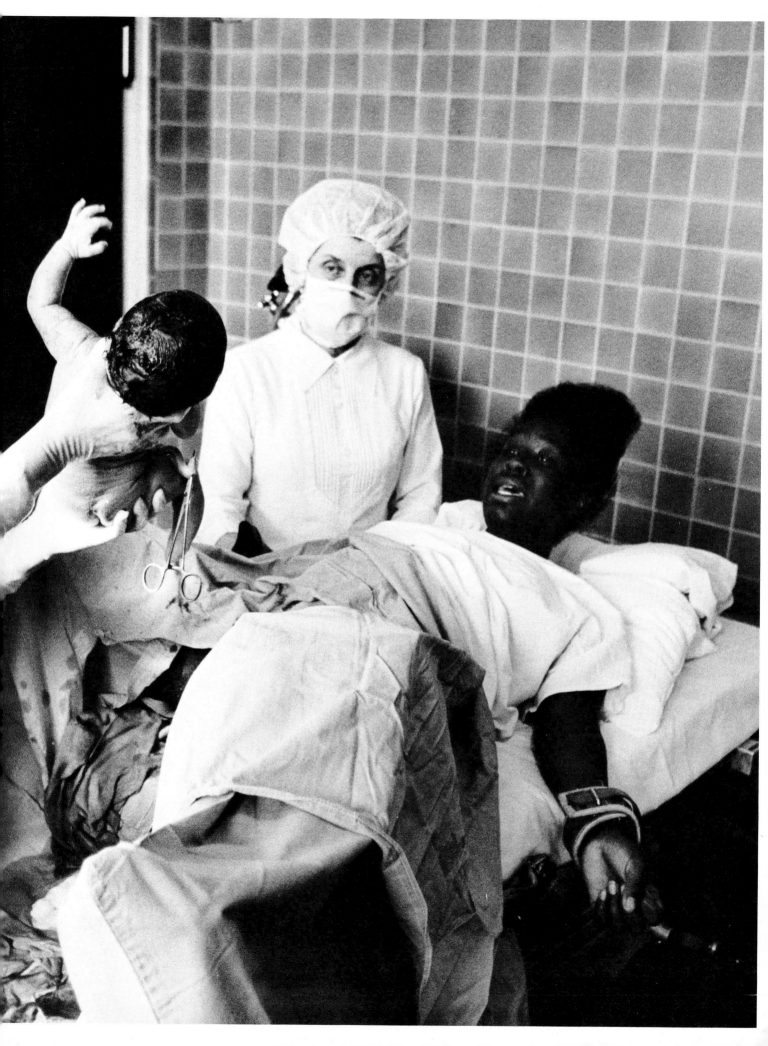

Sharon Epps, age two minutes, a new woman.

Index

Photographer-writer Betty Medsger's own work began at age nine when she picked and sold berries on the small farm where she was raised in western Pennsylvania. Her teen years included such jobs as dishwasher, waitress, governess, and encyclopedia saleswoman. She graduated from Grove City College and then worked for nine years as a newspaper reporter, first for the *Johnstown* (Pa.) *Tribune-Democrat*. As a staff writer for the *Philadelphia Evening Bulletin* and the *Washington Post*, she wrote major length series as well as news stories. Since becoming a free lance photographer-writer two years ago, she researched, reported and produced investigative news documentaries that appeared on WRC-TV, the NBC affiliate station in Washington, D.C., and has written for *Progressive* magazine. A native of R.D. 2, New Florence, Pennsylvania, she now lives with her husband, writer Ben Bagdikian, in Washington, D.C.